HUNGER, CORRUPTION and BETRAYAL

To Larry —
From whom I
learned my
economics —

Oct. 7 '05

ALEJANDRO LICHAUCO

HUNGER, CORRUPTION and BETRAYAL

A Primer on U.S. NEOCOLONIALISM and the PHILIPPINE CRISIS

The story of how the post-war imperialism of the U.S. IMF-WB Group reduced what was the preeminent developing economy in the Asia-Pacific in the fifties to the humanitarian disaster that it is today where 80 percent of the population live in hunger conditions.

An introduction to development economics and the post-war economic history of the Philippines as a neocolony of the U.S.

CITIZENS' COMMITTEE ON THE NATIONAL CRISIS

To Father and his friend, Martin,
who asked for this book
so the world might know of the plight
of his poor in this only
Christian nation in Asia

Pope John Paul said the continuing plight of the Third World was caused directly by peoples and groups who wanted to keep developing countries poor.

The unbalanced development taking place at present and posing the greatest threat to the stability of the world– where the rising material standards of some are in stark contrast with the deepening poverty and misery of others– is not the result of uncontrolled forces, but of decisions made by individuals and groups, he said.

-- Imperialists blamed for havenots' plight
Philippine Journal, June 9, 1989

CONTENTS

ABOUT THE AUTHOR

ALEJANDRO LICHAUCO, political economist and member of the Philippine Bar, is a prominent figure in the nationalist movement. He started his career in nationalist advocacy in the '50s when he joined the Nationalist Citizens Party of Claro M. Recto. In the '60s he became a charter member of the Movement for the Advancement of Nationalism (MAN) which he served as its executive vice-chairman.

In 1970 Lichauco was elected to represent the 1st district of Rizal in the '71 Constitutional Convention. In the convention he submitted a paper on U.S. imperialism in the Philippines. A week after martial law was declared, Lichauco was arrested as he left the convention floor and detained at Camp Crame as a political prisoner. He was charged with subversion for his activities in MAN and for his paper on American imperialism. His paper on American imperialism was published by the Monthly Review Press of N.Y. as the *Lichauco Paper.*

Lichauco was among the 12 delegates who refused to sign the martial law Constitution for which he was placed under house arrest after his release from detention.

Following Edsa 1, Lichauco turned to writing and among his principal books are *Towards a New Economic Order and the Conquest of Mass Poverty* (1986), *Nationalist Economics* (1988) and *The Philippine Crisis* (1992). His writings have focused on the historical connection between U.S. imperialism and mass poverty in the Philippines. Last year, he filed a paper with the Senate outlining the case for debt repudiation.

Lichauco graduated from Harvard College with the degree of B.A. in economics and from the Harvard Law School with the degree of Bachelor of Laws. He was at one time policy director of the Philippine Chamber of Industries, director of the Institute of Economic Studies of Araneta University, senior consultant to the Congressional Economic Planning Office and head of the policy research department of the National Economic Council (now NEDA).

He is married to the former Maria Teresa Hontiveros of Capiz, Capiz.

AN OVERVIEW AND WHY THIS PRIMER

In 1957, the World Bank issued the result of a comparative study made on several Asian Third World economies in the Far East. The study covered the economies of the Philippines, South Korea, Indonesia, Thailand, Singapore, Malaysia and Burma (now Myanmar). The conclusion of the study was that the Philippines and Myanmar were the only economies worth talking about. The rest were dismal prospects.

These were the words of the World Bank in describing the performance and prospect of the Philippine economy in the '50s.

> In the 1950s, the Philippines was the best performer among East Asian economies and was widely regarded as the most promising for the long run... The Philippines has achieved a rapid rate of economic growth in the post-war period since 1949. Production has continued to grow at an average annual rate of 7 percent, despite the disrupting effects of the HUK movement, which hampered economic activity until 1952... By comparison with most underdeveloped countries, the basic economic position is favorable. Through a comparative high level of expenditure on education, transport. . .and industrial plants. . .the Philippines has achieved a position in the Far East second only to Japan. ("RP, Myanmar Asia's economic leaders in the Fifties. . ."*Bulletin,* May 12, 1993)

And then the Fall
and the hunger.

In 2003, forty-six years after the glowing WB report on the Philippines, the Food and Nutrition Research Institute of the Department of Science and Technology (FNRI-DOST) released an official finding that 8 out of 10 households in the Philippines are living under hunger conditions.

The mutation from a nation with the best performing economy in the region – "second only to Japan" - to one in the grip of mass hunger is a catastrophe of colossal proportion which can't be ignored by those engaged in development economics and who seek to untangle the mystery of why poor nations remain poor – or why nations once so promising have turned over time to be excessively poor.

The *Philippine crisis* is a grotesque aberration in a region of the world which is home to the *Asian economic miracle* and the factors behind that aberration should be understood, for reasons too obvious to be discussed, by both Filipinos and the international community.

The need to discuss those factors has assumed an urgency in light of efforts, both in and outside the Philippines, to trivialize the aberration by attributing it to corruption and overpopulation: In brief to an overdose of sin and an overdose of sex.

India, China and Indonesia are live arguments for the proposition that corruption and overpopulation need not deter nations from producing an *economic miracle*. Those three most populous nations in this planet have been consistently rated as even more corrupt than the Philippines but no one can dispute the fact of their phenomenal economic achievement since the '50s – the decade when the Philippines was rated as "second only to Japan."

The proposition they establish is simply this: corruption and economic progress can walk hand in hand, and the question is, why don't they in the Philippines? Why, in the Philippines, should corruption and deteriorating poverty walk hand in hand?

The spectacular rise of China, India and Indonesia to NIC status since the '50s certainly wasn't achieved because their governments suddenly decided to turn sinless and transparent and the people sexually prudent and restrained. Something else explains their rise, just as something else– other than sin and sex– explains the fall of the Philippines from the best performing economy in this region to a plain case of humanitarian disaster.

The human condition
of the Filipino today.

For that is what the Philippines is today– a plain case of humanitarian disaster.

In terms of the human condition, the figures released by the FNRI-DOST translate into local and international media stories of hungry mothers selling their babies in Nueva Vizcaya; hungry fathers selling their kidneys in Tondo; hungry farmers in rice-rich Nueva Ecija eating field rats; infants of indigent parents dying at the rate of one a day at the pediatric ward of the Philippine General Hospital as "doctors and nurses fight emotional battles each day while helplessly watching... because the parents cannot afford to buy medicines and save their children;" mothers smothering their children, and then committing suicide because life has become unbearable and the future can only be more so; millions of Filipinas put in the auction block of the slave trade in the capitals of Europe; millions of parents leave home and family to seek employment abroad to escape the hunger at home even as child mendicants proliferate in the streets and become as common a sight as uncollected garbage.

One can go on endlessly reciting a litany of human wretchedness.

Truth is, this "only Christian nation in Asia," has been reduced to an island of human wreckage to whom no law and morality exist except the jungle law and morality of physical survival.

To be sure, however, the Fall didn't happen overnight. It was a process which began in the '60s in the course of which the nation went through landmark and, to many, traumatic events that would have been inconceivable in the '50s – from martial law and one-man dictatorship to people power revolts which have unseated two sitting presidents.

Table 1 records the history of the nation's economic performance since the '50s. It explains the chain of tumultuous events that started with the decade of the '60s. The figures graphically illustrate the fall from economic preeminence in the '50s to humanitarian disaster today.

Table 1
Average annual growth rate of GDP in %

1950s	7.0
1960-70	5.1
1970-79	6.2
1980-90	1.0
1990-2002	3.5

Source: WB, *World Development Report*, 1981, 2004. Figure for 1950 taken from cited *Bulletin* story on WB report of '57.

Note the following:

(1) For twenty-two years– from 1980 to 2002 (and for that matter to the present, or a period of 24 years)– the economy has been in a virtual state of stagnation, posting an average annual growth rate of between 1 percent and 3.5 percent, or something less than 2.4 percent a year for 22 years. In the meanwhile, population has risen from 45 million to 82 million.

(2) *Over the 40-year period spanned by the '60s to the present, annual growth rate has averaged only some 4 percent– far below the 7 percent registered by the country in the Fifties when the peso-dollar rate was only at P2:$1.*

That's what explains the hunger.

This primer is about the reasons behind the nation's economic stagnation and descent to hunger since the '60s – the factors behind the figures in the table.

They are reasons immeasurably more perverse and ominous than the corruption to which the hunger is popularly attributed because those reasons have to do with an economic ideology long and repeatedly condemned as evil by the Vatican since it issued its encyclical *Quadragesimo Anno* in 1931– a severe moral condemnation of free trade and laissez-faire capitalism, and which Ninoy Aquino pledged to eliminate should he be placed in a position to do so.

But behind the malevolent ideology is a grand design crafted by the U.S. government in 1946– and incorporated in what is known as the *Dodds Report* - to preserve the Philippines as a raw material economy in order to service the raw material requirements of Japan's factories. It was a geopolitical plan that imposed a division of labor between two Asian countries under the U.S. sphere of influence. And the plan could be accomplished only by imposing the evil of free trade on the Philippines while allowing Japan to adopt the most rigorous form of economic protectionism because that was the only way Japan– or any struggling non-industrial economy for that matter– could industrialize.

The Philippine humanitarian disaster represents the triumph in this "only Christian nation in Asia" of a pernicious economic doctrine and of a malevolent design by a lone superpower to preserve– through the forcible application of that doctrine– the Philippines as a raw material economy while promoting the industrialization of Japan, for that superpower's own geopolitical purposes.

That's why the real story behind the *Philippine humanitarian disaster* should be told to both the Filipino and international community and told before that disaster takes on a quantum leap as it is now on the verge of doing.

That disaster, this primer argues, should be laid fully and squarely on both the shoulders of the U.S. government and the IMF, on one hand, and collaborating Filipino functionaries, on the other. For the disaster is essentially the story of how the IMF, with the full knowledge and prodding of the U.S. government, enticed, if not coerced, Philippine officialdom to collaborate in undermining the independence and sovereignty of this nation and in pressing, through that officialdom, the very programs and policies to which the disaster may be directly attributed– and, it must be presumed, in full knowledge of the disaster to which those programs and policies directly lead.

This interpretation of the Philippine tragedy accords with findings made by disinterested   bodies of experts on the international economy as to the   role played by the IMF in the making of the Asian crisis. One of those bodies is the Meltzer Commission of the U.S. Congress.

Finding of the Meltzer Commission that the IMF subverts the independence and sovereignty of the nations it assists.

Following the Asian crisis of 1997, the U.S. Congress tasked a group of prominent economists to inquire into the workings and policies of the IMF and to determine the role of that agency in the making of the crisis. The group, known as the Meltzer Commission after the economist Allan Meltzer, who headed it, included former U.S. Secretary of State George Shultz.

In March 2000, the Commission issued its report, known as the *Meltzer Report*.

As reported by an editorial (titled "Fix the Fund) of the *Asian Wall Street Journal* in that paper's issue of May 28, 2001: **"The Meltzer report argues that the IMF undermines the sovereignty and democratic processes of member governments receiving assistance."**

A Finding of Treason.

If the conclusion of the Meltzer Commission has basis, then what it was actually saying was that the IMF induces nothing less than treason in the governments which approach it for assistance, which accepts its conditionalities and through whom those conditionalities are implemented in the loan-recipient countries.

Because if the IMF indeed "undermines the sovereignty and democratic processes of member governments receiving assistance" from it, it can do so only with and through the treasonous collaboration of the national officials with whom the agency deals.

The Meltzer report, however, didn't uncover anything novel. In the Philippines, belief has been widespread, even before the Asian crisis, that the functionaries, known as technocrats, who have represented the government in negotiations with the IMF, have by and large discharged their office with one eye to future employment in the IMF and the World Bank, to which many of them have in fact landed.

As this primer will discuss, in 1991, a group of senators led by Joseph Estrada, Teofisto Guingona, Alberto Romulo and Aquilino Pimentel, Jr., charged key officials of the Aquino government with "consummated treason" for the way they were handling the debt negotiations with the IMF.

The Philippines provides a specific case example persuasively supportive of the conclusion made by the Meltzer report and illustrative of how the IMF not only under-

mines the sovereignty and democratic processes of countries it is supposed to assist, but of how its policy
prescriptions actually work to preserve Third World nations
in poverty and even hunger.

The mass hunger that now grips the nation must be
laid squarely on the treason of the policies pressed on the
Philippines by the U.S.-IMF-WB Group since 1962 and not,
as is commonly supposed, on corruption and population
growth.

The focus on corruption as the issue conceals the issue
of treason.

Unless that fact is acknowledged there can't be any re-
alistic approach to the *Philippine crisis.*

That crisis is fast approaching an explosion point of
unimagined dimension and it is time that elements of
goodwill in the international community and patriotic-na-
tionalist Filipinos join forces to bail out this only Christian
nation in Asia from the horrendous predicament into
which it has been pushed by what Malaysia's Mahathir
described as the *agents of the new colonialism.*

The Philippine tragedy is the story of how the new
colonialism impacted on the most promising and best performing Third World economy in the Far East in the '50s
and reduced it into a colossal disaster which now threatens to become not only a problem for the region but an
international moral scandal as well which puts in question the very right of the IMF-WB Group to remain in
existence.

ALEJANDRO LICHAUCO
Manila
February 21, 2005

1
WHY SHOULD THERE BE MASS HUNGER IN THIS LAND OF PLENTY?

Q. I find the conclusion of the FNRI-DOST (Food and Nutrition Research Institute of the Department of Science and Technology) that 8 out of 10 households in this country are hungry to be shocking and non-believable. I am prepared to accept that there is hunger, but not to the extent alleged by the FNRI-DOST because that finding amounts to *mass hunger*. How can there possibly be *mass hunger* in a land of plenty whose economy is based on agriculture?

A. The answer has to do with jobs and prices. People may live on land so fertile that one can throw a seed anywhere and see it sprout into something he can eat. But if they don't have the means or money with which to buy the products of the land then they simply starve while staring at the mountains of food around them.

The fact of mass hunger may be inferred from the statistics of the government on the level of poverty in this country. It didn't need the FNRI-DOST report to confirm that fact.

According to government figures, 40 percent of Filipinos are poor because they live on a monthly income of less than P1,300 a month– P1,300 a month being the official poverty line. But P1,300 can only buy one cavan of rice. And if one subsists on only one cavan a rice a month you can be sure that he goes to bed hungry. He isn't only poor but hungry and there's a world of difference between the two.

What I am saying is that the poverty line of P1,300 a month established by the government is both arbitrary and unrealistic. That line isn't a poverty line but a hunger line.

What the government has officially acknowledged without admitting it is that at least 40 percent of the nation's population are hungry and not only poor.

But the important point must be stressed that even if one earns as much as P4,000 a month– or 3 times more than the official poverty income of P1,300– he is still hungry, considering the cost of living today. One therefore shouldn't be shocked by the FNRI-DOST finding that 8 out of 10 households are hungry. It's a finding that has in fact come too late because Filipinos have been hungry long before that finding.

As for the notion that our economy is based on agriculture, the fact is that we have ceased to be an agricultural economy. We are neither an industrial nor an agricultural economy. We are now low-tech, low-wage service economy. Ours has become mainly an economy of low-tech service providers, not of producers.

Q. Please illustrate in figures what you have explained so far.

A. I give you a set of figures.

Table 2
Unemployment (%) and peso-dollar rate

	1980	1985	1990	2000	2003
Unemployment rate					
	4.3	7.1	8.1	10.1	10.1
Peso to the dollar					
	P7.5	18.6	24.3	44.19	54.2

Source: ADB, Key Indicators April 1985, 2004

As of 2005, the unemployment rate had reached 12% and the peso-dollar rate P56:$1.

Table 3
Share of major sectors (%) in GDP

	1980	1990	2003
Agriculture	25.6	21.9	14.5
Manufacturing	25.0	24.8	23.1
Service	38.4	43.6	53.5

Source: ADB, Key Indicators, April 1985, 2004.

Table 2 tells us is that over a period of 23 years, since 1980, joblessness has risen radically along with the rise in prices– the rise in prices being caused by the rise in the peso-dollar rate.

Table 3 explodes the long-standing notion that the Philippine economy is based on agriculture. It isn't anymore. It has transformed into an economy dominated by the service sector. That sector now accounts for a hefty 53.5 percent of the economy, larger than the combined size of the agricultural and manufacturing sectors which stand at 37.6 percent.

Q. How do the figures give an idea of how much prices have risen since 1980?

A. The **peso-dollar rate** in Table 2 tells you that. We are a country importing virtually everything we need and want– from shoe polish to airplanes, and even fighting cocks and basketball players– which means that local prices are very much determined by the peso-dollar rate.

Over the period 1980 to 2003, the peso-dollar rate has risen by more than seven times. So, figure out the comparative cost of prices in 1980 and today.

Q. What caused those figures?

A. Behind those figures and immediately responsible for them is the **deadly mix of import liberalization and devaluation**.

In 1986, following people power, government – at the initiative and insistence of NEDA– was seized with a consuming obsession to eliminate all restraint on imports, and so beginning that year both the system of selective import controls and protective tariffs that had been in force during martial law were progressively dismantled to a point that our tariffs are now down to almost zero and hardly any import controls exists. We have removed import restrictions on many agricultural products that date back to the '50s.

In addition, and to compound matters, the government made devaluation an instrument of policy, *supposedly to promote exports, but in truth to make it progressively cheap for foreign capital to buy into and control the economy*.

In the process of dismantling the tariff and selective import control system over the period 1986 to the present, the government virtually paralyzed the two production legs of the economy– namely, the agricultural and manufacturing legs.

An epidemic of factory closures followed along with the marginalization of agriculture. Our farmers found it increasingly difficult to compete with cheap, subsidized imports of agricultural products, and farming became a losing proposition to many. That explains why the size of the agricultural sector has shrunk considerably, as you note in Table 3 .

Since 1986, when the government started dismantling import controls on farm goods and reducing tariffs on them, there has been no end to farmers' complaint of how their livelihood is being destroyed. Import liberalization has made us a nation of food importers instead of the food producers that we used to be.

The impact of import liberalization on both industry and agriculture has, literally and absolutely, been devastating.

Even giant industrial enterprises which, prior to 1986, seemed invincible, such as **Caltex refining and National Steel Corporation,** have closed shop and a pillar in the agro-industrial sector like **Hacienda Luisita** was marginalized and forced to reduce operations to bare minimum.

Business tycoon John Gokongwei put it starkly when, asked by *Asiaweek* in 1999 on the impact of globalization on the state of the economy, he cited a list industries that, by his count, had already died, among these being the **tire, paper, steel, shoe** and **chemical industries.**

Q. And these industries were killed by imports?

A. Yes. By cheap imports aggravated by devaluation. The damage done by imports was sharply aggravated by the increased cost of production that came with the almost ceaseless rounds of devaluation.

The cases of Hda. Luisita, Caltex Refining, Matsuhita Electric Philippine Corp. and National Steel Corporation as victims of import liberalization

The holocaust that descended on the production sector of the economy was perhaps best expressed by the management of the Hacienda Luisita when it announced that the hacienda was marginalizing operations because of the impact of cheap imports **and** high production cost on its operations.

In a story titled "**Hacienda Luisita hit by globalization**," which appeared in the August 12, 2003 issue of *Today*, the hacienda's management was quoted as saying:

> The HLI said that it has become imperative for the sugar central to reduce its workforce 'to the minimum operational level' in order to prevent cessation of the business.

> It primarily blamed its financial woes on the government's commitment to the World Trade Organization and the General Agreement on Tariff and Trade, which caused the flooding of the local market with imported cheap sugar, as well as the high cost of production (presumably due to devaluation).

The marginalization of Luisita was followed a month later by the announcement of Caltex (Philippines) that it was closing its refinery operations because of, among others, the imports of finished oil products that had flooded the market.

A story titled "**Caltex shuts down Batangas refinery**," which appeared in the September 24, 2003 issue of *Today* quotes the management of Caltex as follows:

> After 50 years of processing crude oil in the country, Caltex Philippines announced the shutdown of its refinery in Batangas effective yesterday (September 23). .. 'Our Batangas refinery was exposed to import competition from those larger and more efficient offshore refineries which significantly eroded our refinery's economic viability.'

Then in May 2004, **Matsushita Electric Philippines Corp.** announced that it was closing shop as local manufacturer of colored TV. The reason given was that:

> Currently, cost competitiveness of locally produced colored TVs has been severely affected by the *lower-*

ing of tariffs on imported products and higher raw ma-
terial costs, among others

Hda. Luisita, Caltex Refining and Matsushita Electric
Corp. are giant pillars in their respective areas of production and when they have had either to marginalize operation
or close shop because of import liberalization and the high
cost of imported raw material brought about by devaluation, then you don't need further proof of how that policy
mix of import lib and devaluation has impacted on the
economy.

Years earlier, in 1999, the nation's largest steel producer
and the oldest in the region, **National Steel Corp.**, was forced
to close its shop in Iligan City, laying off 4000 people, because of cheap imported steel from Russia. (see "National
Steel: Will rehabilitation work this time?" *BusinessWorld,*
September 24, 2003)

The corporation's former chief executive, Armando V.
Armas, citing reasons for the closure, said:

> **Trouble began when the government decided to sell
> NSC to private investors in 1995. It was during that
> period that the government started opening industries
> to foreign competition and selling state-owned com-
> panies.**

The story cites the Tariff Commission finding that:

> **Since the dumping of Russian billets had a negative
> impact on sales and significantly influenced National
> Steel's pricing, it was an important contributory factor
> to the net loss sustained by the company in 1988.**

The story then proceeded to comment that "Even legal
imports gave NSC a run on its money." Then citing the Tariff Commission again:

The commission noted that imported billets increased significantly their market share from 1996 to 1998, and Russia was the dominant player. This, plus the impact of the 1997 Asian financial crisis, eventually forced NSC to close shop.

In fact one can cite case after case of giant enterprises forced to close shop because of import liberalization and devaluation, but there's no need to belabor the point.

And don't forget that many of our manufacturing enterprises were loaded with foreign debt, so that with every devaluation the peso cost of servicing those foreign debts jumped like running kangaroos. That explains the financial crisis into which many corporations, private and public, have fallen, and prominent examples of these are Maynilad, Meralco and Napocor.

Q. Didn't any one object to import liberalization when that program was launched in 1986?

A. It's difficult to name anyone in business who didn't object. Virtually everyone in the business of producing goods, whether manufacturing or farming, objected, and we can start alphabetically with the **American Chamber of Commerce of the Philippines (ACCP)** who, as early as 1986, wrote President Aquino a letter advising her against proceeding with the import liberalization program.

Q. The ACCP objected to import liberalization in 1986?

A. That's right. As early as 1986 ACCP, representing the largest group of foreign investors in the country, warned the Aquino administration that import liberalization would eventually result in the closure of many industries which can't compete with imports because of a number of factors, among these being the high cost of electric power.

Q. And the objection of the American Chamber of Commerce to import liberalization was a matter of record?

A. Yes. Check the *Manila Times* issue of July 3, 1986. In a business section story reporting that the Chamber backs the Aquino government's economic plan but "**says no to import lib**," the *Times* quotes the organization's president, Fred Whiting, as telling the Aquino government that import liberalization "would adversely affect the country's manufacturing sector because the plan would make Philippine-made products uncompetitive with foreign made ones."

The ACCP president continued to say that the import liberalization program "should not be carried out until most industries are financially sound and stable to cope with foreign competition." The organization also cited the high cost of electric power as a major reason why domestic industries are uncompetitive.

Q. And what other foreign groups objected?

A. The **World Bank** (WB) also objected to import liberalization in 1987.

After noting in a confidential memorandum that import liberalization was causing job losses, the WB publicly criticized the technocrats of the Aquino government for the haste with which they were implementing import liberalization.

A story in the September 8, 1987 issue of the *Manila Times* quoted a World Bank official as saying that the program "**was not properly conceived,**" and that "**it was hurriedly put into place by the economic managers.**" ("Import lib plan fails, sets back recovery")

Q. And how about those in government?

A. The **Department of Trade and Industry**, under then DTI Secretary Jose Concepcion, Jr., fiercely resisted import liberalization, along with the late Ramon V. Mitra who then headed the **Department of Agriculture**. Then in 1994, DTI Secretary Rizalino Navarro asked for a deferment of the import liberalization program because his office had found that domestic industries were being undermined by imports. ("DTI urges import leash," *Bulletin*, February 25, 1994).

The **League of Provincial Governors**, headed by the late Bren Guiao, also objected to import liberalization on account of the perceived and anticipated havoc it would work in the rural areas.

Q. Why did the government proceed with import liberalization in the face of the formidable list of parties who objected to it?

A. The program was pressed on the Philippine government by the IMF- and even by the WB despite the latter's finding that import liberalization was undermining local industries.

Q. You mentioned elements in the government who objected to import liberalization.

NEDA's insistence on import liberalization and devaluation

Import liberalization.-

A. Yes, but **the program was vigorously pushed by the National Economic Development Authority (NEDA)** and in the end NEDA'S views prevailed. NEDA after all is supposed to be the agency of government particularly tasked to formulate and recommend development programs and policies.

Q. What reasons did NEDA give for pressing the Aquino government to push through with import liberalization?

The misrepresentations made by NEDA in justifying its policy of import liberalization

Solita Monsod, chair of NEDA then, argued that import liberalization would make domestic industries competitive. She cited the cases of the Asian NIC's who she claimed became NICs because of import liberalization.

That, of course, was like arguing that if one pitted a lightweight against a heavyweight, the lightweight would eventually begin fighting like a heavyweight. But common sense tells us that the lightweight is bound to wind up in a coma.

This was what Monsod said in justifying the program she was assiduously pushing:

> Monsod cited the outstanding achievement of Taiwan and South Korea as examples of countries which improved their local products through import liberalization. . .
>
> Monsod said that had these countries not adopted free trading as a major economic policy, it would still be in a similar condition as the Philippines. ("All import controls to be lifted – Monsod," *Manila Times,* July 26, 1986)

Q. Is it true that the Asian NICs took to import liberalization as Monsod represented they did?

A. On the contrary, the Asian NICs were notorious for the practice of strictly restricting their imports. The Asian NICs came to be what they are because of a development strategy notorious for steep and rigorous barriers they erected against foreign goods. That strategy is called *mercantilism–*

the original name for protectionism– which is the opposite of the free trade espoused by NEDA.

In fact, in 1979, a U.S. congressional task force made a survey of trade practices in Asia and found that America's experience with the trade restrictions of Japan were being duplicated in the "New Japans" of Asia, notably South Korea and Taiwan.

This was the finding of the U.S. congressional task force on the restrictive trade practices of South Korea and Taiwan:

> The two nations impose numerous import restrictions on U.S. and other nations' goods on grounds that they are developing economies. Yet they have – to a large extent – graduated into the ranks of developed economies and special protection is no longer justifiable. ("U.S. warns of rising Asian imports," *Bulletin*, February 18, 1979, a UPI dispatch).

South Korea and Taiwan in fact modeled their respective industrialization strategy on Japan. That's why those two countries have been alluded to as the "New Japans."

Q. And what was Japan's development strategy?

A. Following is *Newsweek's* description of the **Japanese developmental strategy** as told in a story titled "Japan Ready to Deal?" which appeared in one of that magazine's issues in the '70s:

> Since World War 11, Japan has built a high standard of living by stimulating export, subsidizing domestic producers, *and refusing to import any manufactured goods it could possibly live without. As a result only 20 percent of Japan's foreign purchases are finished products, compared with 53 percent for the U.S. and 66 percent for West Germany.*

NEDA on devaluation.–

Q. How about devaluation? What is your basis for saying that NEDA pushed the Aquino administration to devaluation, and, if so, what reason did it have for doing so?

A. As early as 1987, NEDA already kept pressing the government to devalue on the theory that devaluation, by cheapening the peso, would make Philippine exports cheap in the international market and therefore attractive to foreign buyers.

The *Manila Chronicle*, in the March 4, 1987 issue of that paper, carried a story titled "Neda chief bats for devaluation." It quotes Monsod as arguing that "The peso-dollar rate has to be undercut to make our exports more competitive."

Then in the June 27, 1988 issue of *BusinessWorld*, Monsod was reported to have repeated the devaluation argument and to have proposed that "Government should allow market forces to dictate the levels of interest rates and the peso's value."

The June 28, 1988 issue of the *Manila Times*, carried the story titled "Lower peso to induce exports– Monsod."

In November 23, 1989, the *Chronicle* carried a story titled "Neda bats for lower peso value."

So you see that starting 1987, NEDA kept pressing the administration to devalue on the theory that devaluation would be good for exports.

WHAT WAS WRONG WITH
NEDA'S THEORY ON DEVALUATION
AND IMPORT LIBERALIZATION

Q. Please summarize what you think was wrong with NEDA'S theory on devaluation and import liberalization?

The theory on **devaluation** is just that– plain theory, and false theory at that because it contradicts and has been disproved by actual experience. We have been devaluating since 1962– when we devalued from P2:$1 to P3.90:$1– but our international trade position far from improving simply kept deteriorating along with the deterioration of the peso and the debt problem. Today, the peso-dollar rate has reached the astronomical high of P56:$1, and yet our economy and our exports are even less competitive than they were before we devalued in 1962.

The theory overlooked the fact that devaluation as a policy to promote exports makes sense only if you have a broad range of goods– particularly industrial goods– to export to begin with, and not when your exports consist in the main of raw material and non-manufactured goods or semi-processed materials.

THE POINT, HOWEVER, IS THAT DEVALUATION APPARENTLY WAS PRESSED ON OUR GOVERNMENT BY THE IMF-WB – AND SECONDED BY NEDA – FOR ONE PURPOSE AND ONE PURPOSE ONLY: THAT IS, TO MAKE IT INCREASINGLY CHEAPER FOR FOREIGN INVESTORS TO BUY INTO AND CONTROL THE ECONOMY– *EVEN IF THAT MEANT DRIVING THE MASSES TO OUTRIGHT HUNGER.*

With respect to **import liberalization,** the theory of NEDA was that it would stimulate our domestic industries into global competitiveness when what it actually did was to kill the local industries, including agriculture.

NEDA overlooked the fact that when an underdeveloped, non-industrialized economy opens up to imports on a liberal, free trading basis– particularly imports from advanced industrial economies, like the U.S., China and the Asian NICs– the practical impact is analogous to pitting one's flyweight industries against the foreign heavyweights and common sense will tell you what happens to the former. Instead of developing competitiveness they wind up in a stretcher.

Our economy has been living on a stretcher ever since we started the devaluation business in 1962.

Q. And how did the mix of import liberalization and devaluation work out?

A. How the mix of of both policies worked out is there for everybody to see– and feel. Instead of making domestic industries competitive– as Monsod and company claimed it would– import liberalization choked our domestic industries to death.

As for the theory that devaluation would make exports competitive, what it did was to increase both the cost of production and the cost of living and any advantage which devaluation might have given to exports has been overwhelmed by the negative consequences it had for production cost and by the adverse social consequences it brought about.

As this primer will discuss, **an in-house study of the IMF in 1988 concluded that devaluation, which the IMF had pressed on the Philippines since 1962, has worked havoc on the poor of the Philippines.**

But notwithstanding that, both the IMF-WB and NEDA continued to press for a policy of devaluation.

Q. IF IT IS TRUE THAT A STAFF STUDY OF THE IMF
ACKNOWLEDGED AS EARLY AS 1988 THAT DEVALU-
ATION HAS BEEN BAD FOR THE PHILIPPINES, WHY
DID NEDA AND THE IMF-WB CONTINUE TO INSIST
ON DEVALUATION?

A "scheme to destroy industries" of the
Philippine Institute of Development Studies or PIDS.

A. NEDA has been manned largely by economists recruited
from the U.P. School of Economics, and that school since
the '60s has identified itself with free trade economics and
the policy of devaluation on the theory that devaluation will
improve the nation's international trade situation.

Early in the administration of Corazon C. Aquino, U.P
economists grouped together as the **Philippine Institute of
Development Studies (PIDS)** and prepared a development
plan for NEDA. That plan was criticized by a noted industrialist, who would eventually become a member of the
Aquino cabinet, as tantamount to a "scheme to destroy industries."

Q. Who was that industrialist and member of the Aquino
cabinet who accused the PIDS of scheming to destroy the
nation's industries?

A. Ceferino Follosco. Follosco at the time was writing a column for *Business Day* and it was in the June 13, 1986 issue
of that paper that his column appeared, aptly titled **"A
scheme to destroy industries."**

I quote pertinent portions of the column which, in the
light of subsequent developments, have assumed the nature of a prophecy:

Much has been discussed about the IMF-imposed Import Liberalization Program. . . We understand the

objective of IMF, but what alarms us is the recommendation of the PIDS paper on "Economic Recovery For
Long Term Growth," prepared mostly by UP profes-
sors and is being used by NEDA as a basis for
discussions.

The paper in general is too agro-oriented instead of being a balanced agro-industrial development strategy...

What PIDS expects to do is to destroy (through import
liberalization) in one sweep the industrial infrastructure
built over the last 40 years and build a new structure
dependent on agriculture.

**Q. Do you think that the members of PIDS who wrote the
plan they recommended to NEDA did so with the inten-
tion of destroying the nation's industries?**

A. The members of PIDS who authored the plan they recommended to NEDA might just have been victims of what
the late Renato Constantino described as *the miseducation of
the Filipino*. At the very least they were miseducated into
thinking that the welfare and progress of this country de-
pends on destroying its industries.

Q. And did NEDA adopt the plan recommended by PIDS?

A. Judging by the aggressiveness with which NEDA pushed
for import liberalization and the impact of the program on
industry, I would say that the PIDS plan became the basis of
the government's development plan that was submitted to
the country's international creditors in Tokyo.

Reaction of the Japanese Government
to the NEDA Plan in 1987

It is revealing that when the Philippine government
presented its development plan in Tokyo, the Japanese government commented that the growth targets of the plan

weren't likely to be achieved because the plan was biased against industry in favor of agriculture.

The matter was reported by the *Business Day* in its February 12, 1987 issue. I quote pertinent portions of the story, which was titled "Japan doubts RP growth targets..."

The cited paragraphs below of the story on the reaction of the Japanese government to the development plan submitted by the Philippine government leave no room for doubt as to the bias against industrialization of the NEDA plan.

> Japan has expressed doubts about the Philippine ability to achieve its target 1987-1992 average growth rate of about 6.5 percent, as shown in a Japanese delegate report at the recent meeting of the Consultative Group of the country's creditor governments and multilateral agencies.

> Japan has also cautioned the Philippines against concentrating on agriculture at the expense of industrial development.

> The (Philippine) plan's thrust toward agricultural and rural-based development should not be done at the expense of developing the industrial sector, the (Japanese) delegation report says.

That was the Japanese government's reaction to the NEDA plan as far back as 1987. It was literally an accusation that the NEDA plan was a plan done "at the expense of developing the industrial sector."

Q. And all that explains the hunger?

A. That and the policy of devaluation also insisted on by NEDA.

But we must dig deeper and search for the reason that would plausibly explain why NEDA– the agency charged with framing the development plans of the government– insisted on a development strategy that, as critics of the plan had predicted, would destroy industries; **particularly so after an in-house staff study of the IMF in 1988 had acknowledged that the policies which the IMF had been pressing on our governments since 1962– particularly devaluation– had backfired against the poor.**

Q. Was there such a study by the IMF staff?

IMF staff study in 1988 admitted that
the policy prescriptions pressed
by the IMF on the Philippines since 1962
had aggravated the poverty problem.

A. There was and it was made public by both local and international media. In a story titled "IMF programs hurt the poor," the June 2, 1988 issue of the *Manila Chronicle* published an *Associated Press* dispatch, pertinent paragraphs of which I quote below:

> A report from the International Fund acknowledges that poor people have been hurt by policies it has prescribed on Third World countries with the support of the United States.

> In the past, the IMF has stressed that countries would be worse off if they delay policies, such as devaluation of currencies and cuts in government spending, usually required as a condition for IMF loans.

> The report chose seven sample countries whose governments in recent years have adopted adjustment programs in order to get loans from the Fund: Chile, Dominican Republic, Ghana, Kenya, *Philippines*, Sri Lanka, and Thailand.

Q. Were there other media stories on that IMF staff study?

A. Yes. *Malaya's* issue of June 13, 1988, carried a story titled: "IMF policies penalize the poor– confirmed by in-house study." The opening paragraphs of that story, under the by-line of Juan V. Sarmiento, Jr. of the Philippine News and Features, read as follows:

> A study by the International Monetary Fund (IMF) whose policies have long been criticized for making life difficult for Filipinos, admits that the Fund- supported programs in the Philippines have indeed adversely affected the majority poor.
>
> 'The implications of Fund-supported adjusted programs for poverty,' and IMF study of May 1988, examined the impact of policy measures adopted under Fund-supported adjustment program on poverty in the Philippines as well as on six other countries. . .
>
> *The IMF study says that devaluation was one adjustment policy in the Philippines that proved costly to the poor. It found that in countries like the Philippines, devaluation imposed immediate cost on the urban poor who are engaged in the production of non-tradables and goods using imported inputs.*

The story also noted that:

> *"From 1963 to 1985, IMF had overseen 17 standby agreements and one extended fund-facility for the Philippines.*

Q. What's the relevance of that story to our discussion and why the reference to the years "1963 to 1985?"

A. In 1962 the administration of President Diosdado Macapagal devalued the peso from its original rate of P2:$1 to P3.90 and dismantled the system of foreign exchange and import controls (**Forex**) which had been in force since 1950.

Those two decisions constituted what was called the De-control Program.

The peso was devalued and Forex was lifted because that was the only way the Philippines could obtain a $300 million loan it had applied for from the IMF. Since then the Philippine economy has operated under the supervision of the IMF which, in exchange for every loan, has pressed the government for one devaluation after another and insisted that our economy be kept open to imports as much as possible.

Hence, from an original peso-dollar rate of P2:$1 in 1961, that rate has ballooned to its present P56:$1. And from a foreign debt of $150 million in 1961, we now reel under a debt load of $56 billion.

The **Table 4** graphically illustrates the rate at which the peso has devalued simultaneously with the rise in the nation's foreign debt since 1961 – the year before when, in 1962, we first submitted ourselves to the supervision of the IMF:

Table 4
Peso-Dollar rate and foreign debt 1961-present

	1961	1962	1965	2005
Debt	$150 M		$600 M	$56 B
P:$ rate	P 2:$1	3.90:1	3.90:1	P56: $1

In spite of the finding made by the aforementioned IMF in-house staff study, however, NEDA has kept on espousing a policy of devaluation. Since the Aquino administration, NEDA has aggressively pushed for the devaluation of the peso.

Q. Was the Decontrol Program of 1962 an example of what you call the "deadly mix of import liberalization and devaluation?"

A. Yes. It was our first experience with that deadly mix in the hands of the IMF. We liberalized importations by dismantling import controls and devalued.

Q. Then why has the IMF continued to press for devaluation even after its own staff in 1988 had acknowledged that devaluation has worked havoc on the lives of the poor?

THE REAL REASON FOR DEVALUATION:
TO ENABLE FOREIGN INVESTORS TO BUY INTO
AND CONTROL THE ECONOMY
AS CHEAPLY AS POSSIBLE
– EVEN IF THAT MEANT DRIVING
THE MASSES TO HUNGER

A. IF DESPITE AN IMF STAFF STUDY IN 1988 ACKNOWLEDGING THAT DEVALUATION HAS BEEN A MISTAKE AND HAS WORKED HAVOC ON THE POOR, THE IMF-WB GROUP HAS CONTINUED TO PRESS FOR DEVALUATION NONETHELESS, THE ANSWER IS, AND CAN ONLY BE, THAT DEVALUATION MAKES IT CHEAPER FOR FOREIGN INVESTORS TO BUY INTO THE PHILIPPINE ECONOMY.

THE REASON IS THAT WITH EVERY DEVALUATION OF THE PESO, THE PURCHASING   POWER OF THE DOLLAR OVER THE ECONOMY BECOMES STRONGER.

FOR EXAMPLE, AT AN EXCHANGE RATE OF P2:$1, ONE DOLLAR CAN ONLY BUY TWO PESOS WORTH OF GOODS AND SERVICES IN THE PHILIPPINES. BUT AT AN EXCHANGE RATE OF P56:$1, THE SAME DOLLAR CAN PURCHASE FIFTY-SIX PESOS WORTH OF PHILIPPINE GOODS AND SERVICES.

THAT'S HOW CHEAP OUR ECONOMY HAS BECOME FOR FOREIGN INVESTORS SINCE THE FIRST

DEVALUATION OF THE PESO IN 1962. AND THAT EX-
PLAINS THE HUNGER.

IT IS OBVIOUS THAT IN PRESSING FOR DEVALU-
ATION, THE IMF-WB DIDN'T HAVE THE WELFARE OF
OUR ECONOMY IN MIND. WHAT IT HAD IN MIND
APPARENTLY WAS TO PROMOTE THE INTEREST OF
FOREIGN INVESTORS EVEN IF IT KNEW THAT DE-
VALUATION WOULD MAKE THE ALREADY
IMPOVERISHED MASSES EVEN MORE IMPOVER-
ISHED - AS THE IMF STAFF STUDY ACKNOWLEDGED
IN 1988.

Q. But that still doesn't fully answer the question: Why
would the IMF-WB insist on policies which they know
undermine Philippine development?

A. That's one of the questions this book will answer.

2

THE NATURE AND ESSENCE
OF THE PHILIPPINE CRISIS

Q. Before all else, please explain what you mean by the *Philippine crisis*. Specifically, what is the nature of that crisis? It seems so all-encompassing that one is at a loss on how to start dealing with it.

A. The *Philippine crisis* is, as you say, all-encompassing. It is the compound and sum total of numerous crises.

Q. Please elaborate.

A. We have, for example, what they call the crisis of law and order and the crisis of the justice system; the crisis of our political institutions and the economic order; the moral crisis; the crisis of health care; the crisis of the educational system, the crisis of the peso, the crisis of the agricultural and industrial sectors, the crisis of the military and so on.

All these particular crises in turn stem from problems that seem to have become insoluble, like the problem of poverty and unemployment, of high prices, access to education and health care, the problem of the deficit and the bankruptcy of the government; the foreign debt; corruption in all places, from the barangays to Malacanang and from the police precincts to the Supreme Court, the problem of insurgency and secessionism, and so on..

Name any conceivable problem of state, and you have it. That's the *Philippine crisis* and that's why it seems unsolvable.

Q. Then how do you even start attacking the crisis? Where and how do we begin?

A. I suggest we start with your question on what is **the essence and nature of the crisis.**

**The mortal mix of corruption and poverty and
consequent loss of popular confidence in government
and the electoral process as instruments of change**

The mortal mix of two problems are: (1) a **massive poverty** so intense as to have actually degenerated into a problem of mass hunger; and (2) **a massive corruption** as massive as the massive poverty.

That mix has resulted in the loss of popular confidence in government and the electoral process as instruments of change.

That mix plus the consequent loss of popular faith in government constitute, in my view, the nature and essence of the *Philippine crisis.*

Q. And don't you find that mix in other countries?

A. No. That mix is unique to the Philippines. Elsewhere corruption goes hand in hand with progress and rising prosperity along with continued faith in government. Here, in contrast, corruption goes hand in hand with worsening poverty. That in turn has led to the popular loss of confidence in the political system itself, including democracy as a system of governance.

For example, four years ago, Transparency International released a corruption index and that index rated China, Thailand, Vietnam and Indonesia as more corrupt and prone to bribery than the Philippines.

The Philippines in that rating ranked 54 while China ranked 58, Thailand 68, India 72, and Vietnam 75 – the higher numbers indicating a higher level of corruption. (see "Corruption damaging emerging economies," AP dispatch, *Manila Standard*, January 22, 2000).

And yet all those countries without exception have been galloping economically while the Philippines hasn't only failed to gallop but is now in coma.

Q. Do you have evidence for that?

A. Yes. Take a look at the figures in Table 5:

Table 5
GDP Growth performance (%)
of countries rated as corrupt, 1996-2001

Year	1996	1997	1998	1999	2000	2001
China	9.6	8.8	7.8	7.1	8.0	7.3
India	8.1	4.8	6.5	6.1	4.0	5.4
Indonesia	7.8	4.7	13.1	0.8	4.9	3.3
Thailand	5.9	1.4	10.5	4.4	4.6	1.8
Vietnam	9.3	8.2	5.8	4.8	6.8	n.a
Philippines	5.8	5.2	0.6	3.4	4.4	3.2

SOURCE: ADB, *Key Indicators* 2002

According to the May 8, 2004 issue of the *Economist*, while Vietnam had a poverty level of 58 percent in 1993, by 2002 that level had fallen to 29%. In other words, Vietnam despite the corruption, managed to reduce its poverty rate by half within the space of ten years.

China and India have always been scourged by corrupt governments. But look where they are today. They are regional superpowers not only in the economic but in the military sense as well, although both continue to be hounded by corruption as they have always been.

Elsewhere, as the figures show, countries no matter how plagued by corruption have governments which continue basically to command the confidence of people. The reason is that those governments have managed to compensate for their corruption with economic progress.

In the Philippines, the mix of corruption and poverty has led to a total loss of confidence in government as well as in the political institutions identified with representative democracy and the economic system. Elections are no longer seen as a means by which governance can be improved and by which the masses can improve their lives.

Q. Again the question: How do we get out of the crisis?

A. If you believe that the nature and essence of the crisis is the deadly mix of corruption and poverty, then the obvious answer is to identify the root of that mix and stamp that root out.

3

ROOTS OF THE PHILIPPINE CRISIS

THE FAILURE TO CARRY OUT AN INDUSTRIAL REVOLUTION AND TRANSFORM INTO AN ASIAN NIC OR *NEWLY INDUSTRIALIZED COUNTRY*

Q. What in your view is at the root of what you call the deadly mix of corruption and poverty?

A. Let me begin with certain statistics. **Tables 6 and 7** below tell us how other countries have avoided the mix of corruption and poverty. They have avoided that mix by engineering the most important revolution to which peoples and governments of a Third World country can and should aspire.

Q. And what is that revolution?

A. An industrial revolution. Another name for it is industrialization. Through industrialization, countries once poorer than the Philippines– South Korea, Malaysia, Thailand, Singapore, and Indonesia– have either lifted themselves out of poverty or are fast lifting themselves out of it. All these are now NICs or newly industrialized countries, a coveted status which the Philippines has yet to earn.

Q. How did the Asian NICs become NICs?

A. By making it a policy to do so, and that policy is reflected in the rate at which they developed their manufacturing sector. The following tables illustrate that.

The figures in Tables 6 and 7 explain how our Asian neighbors avoided the deadly mix of corruption and poverty– the mix which is at the heart of the Philippine crisis.

Note the figures carefully and see just how the Philippines compares.

Table 6
Average annual rate of growth (in %)
of the manufacturing sector

	1960-70	'70-79	'80-90	'90-'02
China	n.a.	n.a.	10.8	11.9
Indonesia	3.3	12.5	12.8	5.9
Malaysia		12.4	9.3	8.8
Thailand	11.0	11.4		
South Korea	17.6	17.8	12.1	7.6
Philippines	6.7	6.7	0.2	3.1

Source: WB, World Development Report, 1981, 2004

Table 7
Share/size of manufacturing sector as a percent
of Gross Domestic Product (GDP)

	1980	2001
Indonesia	11.6	26.1
Malaysia	n.a	32.1
Thailand	21.5	33.5
South Korea	29.7	30.0
China	44.2	44.4
Philippines	25.7	22.8

Source: ADB Key Indicators 2002

Note two things: One is the rate at which the manufacturing sector of the countries grew over time. And the other is the increase in the size of the manufacturing sector expressed as a percentage of the economy.

Both tables illustrate the rate at which our neighbors have been industrializing. They also illustrate how, in contrast, the Philippines has been left behind, and even **retrogressed.**

Q. In what way has the Philippines retrogressed?

A. Look at **Table 7** again. It shows that in 1980 our manufacturing sector constituted more than 25 percent of the
economy. But by year 2001, that sector had conspicuously
shrunk in size to less that 23 percent of the economy. In
contrast, the rest saw their respective manufacturing sector
increase in size as a percent of their economy. The increase
was most prominent and sizeable in Indonesia and Thailand.

What **Table 7** illustrates is that we haven't only failed
to advance toward industrialization but that we actually
started retreating from the goal; that is, **we have been de-
industrializing instead of industrializing.**

Tables 6 and 7 explain how Asian countries have managed to avoid the mix of corruption and poverty. In those
countries, to repeat, corruption and rising prosperity walk
hand in hand. In the Philippines, on the other hand, it is
corruption and poverty, and now hunger, that walk hand in
hand.

Q. Please explain what you mean by *de-industrialization.*

A. It simply means that instead of adding to the stock or
number of industrial enterprises in the country, we have been
losing them. In brief, industries that used to exist before
have already died.

Q. Please give examples.

A. In 1999 businessman John Gokongwei was interviewed
by *Asiaweek* on the impact of globalization on the Philippine economy and this was what he said:

> "Nearly all our industries will die. Our tire industry, shoe
> industry, steel, textile and paper industries, for example, are
> dead. (*Asiaweek* Feb. 19, 1999).

Five years after that prediction, long-established and seemingly invincible pillars of the economy have either closed shop or been marginalized– all victims of import liberalization.

We have mentioned four casualties of import liberalization– Hacienda Luisita, Caltex refining, Matsushita Electric Philippines Corp. and National Steel Corp.– which serve as prominent examples of the devastation wrought by import liberalization and devaluation on the economy. The fate of these giant enterprises is perhaps the most dramatic illustration of what de-industrialization means.

Explaining the stellar performance of the economy in the '50s and its fall beginning in the '60s.

Q. But how did we manage to have industries in the first place and how come many of them are now dead as businessman Gokongwei reports it?

A. We shall discuss that at length in the section on import and foreign currency controls and our introduction to industrialization in the '50s.

At this point, it should suffice to say that those industries were the result of an entire decade of the economic protectionism which came with the decision to install a system of import and foreign currency (exchange) controls in the '50s. Throughout that decade the right of citizens and residents to exchange their pesos for dollars and to import any thing they wanted was extensively and rigorously restricted. That restriction operated to provide capitalists, both Filipinos and non-Filipinos, the incentive to establish industries producing goods whose importation was either limited or banned altogether. That, essentially, was the reason for the emergence of industries – known as import substitution industries- that were simply non-existent before the '50s.

Examples are the manufacture of household appliances, tire, textile, pharmaceuticals, paper, car assembly, oil refining and a broad range of steel products and construction materials.

The extinction of those industries, in turn, was a process that began with the decision in 1962 of the administration of Diosdado Macapagal to dismantle that system of controls and to devalue the peso. That decision comprised what came to be known as the *Decontrol Program of 1962.*

Again, this point will be discussed at length later.

Q. **Your thesis then is that the culprit behind the country's failure to industrialize is the policy of import liberalization or what they call free trade?**

A. Not quite. We have to answer a deeper question, and that is: What force has been behind the policy of import liberalization and free trade all along?

Why, in particular, has a succession of governments since 1986 insisted on applying import liberalization to the point of destroying virtually every industry we had managed to establish during the '50s and making it impossible for the country to industrialize and transform into an NIC?

The way our governments have applied the policy of import liberalization has been tantamount to a methodical and deliberate policy of undermining any and all effort to become an NIC and destroying existing industries, which is what the policy succeeded in doing. And we must understand the reason for that bizarre policy.

Q. **And what do you think explains that policy?**

A. That question takes us to the subject of U.S. neocolonialism: its nature, operation and purposes in the Philippines.

NEOCOLONIALISM

4

HOW U.S. NEOCOLONIALISM HAS PREVENTED THE PHILIPPINES FROM INDUSTRIALIZING AND PRESERVED IT AS A RAW MATERIAL ECONOMY.

Neocolonialism defined

Q. What is neocolonialism and what is its connection with the *Philippine crisis?*

A. Webster's dictionary defines neocolonialism as *"the policy of a strong nation in seeking political and economic hegemony over an independent nation or extended geographical area without necessarily reducing the subordinate nation or area to the legal status of a colony."*

Another definition of neocolonialism is *"the exploitation of a supposedly independent region (or nation), as by imposing a puppet government."*

Q. How do strong nations accomplish the policy of bringing about puppet governments?

A. Through various modes of interventionism in the affairs of the subordinate nation, such as intervening in the electoral process of the subordinate nation in order to influence the outcome of that process and elect a government that would essentially be the **puppet** of the superior or intervening power.

The subordinate nation is then known as **a neocolony** or a **puppet state** and the superior nation is known as a **neocolonial** power.

Q. Has the U.S. practiced neocolonialism in the Philippines and if so, how has it done that?

A. Since 1946, when the Philippines assumed international status as a sovereign and independent nation, the U.S. has applied policies and practices that converted this country into a *neocolony* of the U.S.

Q. Please give examples of policies and practices applied by the U.S. that have kept and preserved the Philippines as a U.S. *neocolony.*

A. The most important of those practices is that of actively intervening in our presidential elections to make sure that our presidents– and the resulting administrations they head – function essentially as the executors of U.S. aims and policies for this country, whether it is to mount policies that preserve the country as a raw material economy, or to adopt free trade and free market economics as the nation's economic philosophy even if these are so obviously unsuited to our condition, or to allow U.S. forces to establish a military presence and undertake military exercises in Philippine territory even under terms which violate the Constitution, or send troops to Iraq, and otherwise treat America's enemies as our enemies, even if they are in fact our friends or potential friends, and get embroiled in America's international problems and affairs.

Evidence of U.S. interventionism
in the Philippine electoral process.-

Q. What evidence do you have that the U.S. government intervenes in the electoral process and presidential elections in this country?

A. Former President Diosdado Macapagal in an article he wrote for the *Bulletin* in May 21, 1995, categorically stated– and complained– that "The U.S. government was decisive in the choice of the country's presidents since Filipinos elected their presidents...and no candidate for Philippine president opposed by the American government ever won."(see article of Diosdado Macapagal titled *Remedies against poverty*).

But among the most damaging proof of U.S. interventionism in our presidential elections came from an agent of the CIA who was in charge of U.S. operation against then incumbent President Carlos P. Garcia in the elections of 1961. The CIA agent subsequently claimed credit for having created the political coalition that unseated the incumbent Garcia and installed then Vice President Diosdado Macapagal to the presidency.

Q. And who was the CIA agent who publicly claimed credit for having installed former President Diosdado Macapagal to the presidency?

A. The agent's name was Joseph B. Smith and he made the claim in an extensive book he wrote recounting his exploits as a CIA agent in the Philippines and elsewhere. The book's title is *"Portrait of a Cold Warrior,"* and it was published in 1976 by G.P. Putnam's Sons of New York.

Q. Did Smith narrate the ways and means by which the CIA promoted the candidacy of Diosdado Macapagal and how it undermined the re-election bid of then incumbent Carlos P. Garcia?

A. Yes. According to Smith, the strategic objective of the CIA was to keep Garcia from being re-elected. Since there were two opposition parties then– the Liberal Party (LP) and the Progressive Party of the Philippines (PPP)– the CIA felt that the incumbent Garcia and the Nacionalista Party he headed couldn't be defeated unless the two opposition parties were persuaded to coalesce and put up a common candidate. Getting the LP and PPP to coalesce into a *Grand Alliance* then became the principal mission of the CIA. The Agency began working on the coalition to unseat Garcia as early as 1959.

As Agent Smith put it:

> In short, we (CIA) wanted the Progressives to merge with the Liberals so that there would be the kind of organizational base required to win.

> **In 1961, the winning team was Macapagal and Pelaez...The new coalition we started working on after November 1959 swept the elections.**

Q. Was there money involved?

A. Yes. As Smith acknowledged in his book:

> Our election project was approved for $250,000. I used my persuasive talent and finally got Richardson to agree to let me spend $200,000 on the Grand Alliance while he arranged to give $50,000 to Macapagal.

Q. And didn't the CIA know that it was violating Philippine laws when it decided to get involved in the elections of '61?

A. Of course the CIA knew that it was violating Philippine laws in getting involved in our elections but Agent Smith justified the action of the Agency in these words:

> ...I didn't want to interfere in the internal affairs of the Philippines, but that, on the other hand, the country deserved far better leadership than it was getting and anything that anyone could do to further this end I considered a worthwhile cause.

Q. Were there other incumbent or sitting presidents of this country whose presidential aspiration was opposed by the U.S.?

A. Yes. In fact since we first held elections for the presidency in 1945, the U.S. has opposed the bid for reelection of the following sitting presidents: **Sergio Osmena,** Sr., in the elections of '45; **Elpidio Quirino,** in the elections of '53; **Carlos P. Garcia,** in the elections of '61; and **Diosdado Macapagal,** in the elections of '65.

All these sitting presidents were unseated in the elections where they cast their bid for re-election.

In the case of **Ferdinand Marcos,** while the popular impression is that he was unseated by people power, the fact is that the people power was engineered by the U.S. State Department.

Q. And what is your basis for saying that the unseating of Ferdinand Marcos was engineered by the U.S. State Department?

A. Former U.S Secretary of State George Shultz admitted that. Shultz, who was secretary of state when Marcos was unseated, has openly claimed that the U.S. government removed Marcos because "Marcos had refused to undertake the reforms which the U.S. government wanted him to make." (see "U.S. insists on role in the revolution," *Sunday Express,* May 18, 1986)

According to an article written by Robert L. Bartley, editor of the *Wall Street Journal,* which appeared in the December 17, 2002 issue of its sister paper, the *Asian Wall Street Journal,* the "point man" in "engineering the removal of Marcos and the restoration of Democracy in the Philippines", was then Assistant Secretary of State Wolfowitz– the same Wolfowitz involved in the unseating– or political pretermination– of Saddam Hussein.

Q. Were there other presidential aspirants whose bid for the presidency was opposed by the U.S.?

A. Yes. The most prominent of those aspirants was Claro M. Recto, the presiding officer of the Constitutional Convention of 1935.

In the elections of '57, Recto ran for the presidency as candidate of the independent Nationalist Citizens Party (NCP). There were four presidential aspirants in that election. And the CIA focused its operations on Recto. The objective of that operation wasn't only to make sure that Recto lost but that he lost resoundingly and humiliatingly, which was what happened.

The CIA "dirty trick" operation against Recto was described by American author Raymond Bonner in his classic work on the Marcos dictatorship *Waltzing with a Dictator*. In the section related to the CIA operation against Recto, Bonner wrote:

> The CIA set about to destroy Recto...It planted stories that he was a Communist Chinese agent who had been infiltrated into the Philippine senate. To derail Recto's electoral ambitions, the agency prepared packages of condoms, which it labeled 'Courtesy of Claro M. Recto – the people's friend.' The condoms all had pinprick-size holes in them at the most inappropriate place.

So virulent was U.S. hostility against Recto that the effort to destroy him included assassinating him. That too was recounted by author Bonner when he wrote:

> The agency (CIA) went further. The CIA station chief, General Ralph B. Lovett, and the American ambassador, Admiral Spruance, discussed assassinating Recto, going so far as to prepare a substance for poisoning him, an assassination plot that had not been discussed before.

Q. Was there anything in common shared by those candidates who were opposed by the U.S.?

A. Yes. Without exception they all believed in industrializing the Philippines and they set out to do so.

Q. That was the reason why the U.S. opposed their candidacies?

A. Yes.

Q. But why should the U.S. oppose the industrialization of the Philippines?

THE *DODDS* REPORT AND AMERICA'S POST-WAR ANTI-INDUSTRIALIZATION PLAN FOR THE PHILIPPINES

A. The late Dr. Salvador Araneta, while in exile in Canada during martial law, uncovered the existence of a document known as the **Dodds Report**. The document originated from the U.S. State Department in 1946.

According to Araneta, the **Dodds Report** recommended a geopolitical plan which called for the U.S. to develop Japan as the industrial powerhouse in Asia while simultaneously preserving the Philippines as a raw material economy. The recommendations of that document, also according to Araneta, were accepted by the Truman administration.

So incensed was Araneta on uncovering the document that he wrote a book, which he titled *America's Double Cross of the Philippines*. It was in that book that he exposed and denounced the **Dodds Report**. The book, written in Canada in the mid '70s, was launched posthumously in the Philippines a few years ago by members of the Araneta family.

Following are Araneta's words on that document, which appear on page 55 of his cited book:

> The indifferent economic development of the country...was due to America's policy toward Japan and the Philippines. This policy was the result of the *Dodds Report*, which (U.S. President) Truman accepted, and which

had, as its objective, *to make Japan the industrial workshop of Asia and the Philippines a mere supplier of raw materials.*

We do not argue against the wisdom with the means to rehabilitate and allow her to become an industrial country once again...But certainly we can argue against a policy that would make Japan the *exclusive industrialized country in the Far East, for such a policy was most detrimental to the Philippines.*

As a result of this (U.S.) policy industrialization in the Philippines suffered severe setbacks and delay.

Q. What could possibly have been the reason for the decision of the U.S. government to adopt the recommendation of the *Dodds Report*?

A. Apparently, as the Second World War came to a close, the U.S. government made the fateful decision to utilize Japan as its principal base from which to project American economic and military power in the Far East. That understandably required two things, namely: (1) that Japan be kept economically strong and socially stable, which in turn meant allowing and even inducing it to be an industrial state. Japan, of course, was a logical and ideal choice because prior to the war Japan was the only industrialized nation in the Far East and therefore had the intellectual and cultural infrastructure to implement a real industrialization program; and (2) that Japan, a nation bereft of natural resource, had to be assured of a permanent, external source of the materials that would feed the requirements of its industrial factories. That in turn explains the policy to preserve the Philippines a raw material economy.

MODES BY WHICH THE U.S. HAS KEPT THE PHILIPPINES FROM INDUSTRIALIZING

Q. How, after the Philippines had become sovereign and independent, was the U.S. able to implement the recommendation and objective of the *Dodds Report* to preserve

the Philippines as a raw material economy and keep it from industrializing?

Political interventionism.-

A. First, as discussed, by interfering in our presidential elections to make sure that the candidate preferred by the U.S.– which means the candidate who will follow what the U.S. tells him to do– wins the election.

Economic interventionism.-

Second, by then pressing on our presidents– whose election the U.S. has maneuvered and installed in power– **programs and policies** that work to keep our economy open to imports as much as possible and to make sure that no administration ever embarks on any serious program of industrialization such as that adopted by our neighbors.

Other modes of interventionism.-

There are, of course, other modes of interventionism, such as military, cultural, educational and even religious, but for the moment it is political and economic interventionism that concerns us.

Q. By what names have those economic programs and policies been called?

A. They have been called by various names, such as: *free trade, import liberalization, tariffication and globalization. But by whatever name, the* one overriding objective of the policies has been to make sure that the Philippine market is so flooded and overwhelmed by imports as to undermine, if not strangle, any existing industry and make it prohibitive and even impossible for new industries to emerge.

Q. Please enumerate the various programs and policies that have kept our economy wide open to imports and prevented this country from industrializing.

A. I enumerate below the various economic programs and policies which have kept our economy open widely to and unprotected from imports at various stages of our post-war history.

Programs and policies pressed by the U.S.
on the Philippine authorities that have prevented
this country from industrializing.

First, through the policies imposed by the **Bell Trade Act of 1946.** This was the U.S. law which laid down the conditions under which the Philippines was to receive desperately needed war compensation and financial assistance after the last world war. **Among the conditions imposed by that Act was that the Philippines shall allow the imports of U.S. goods without any limitation whatsoever, free of tariffs and any form of restrictions.** That was the so-called *free trade provision of the Act;*

Second, through the policies represented by the **IMF conditionalities** under which we have been living since 1962 when the **Decontrol Program** of Diosdado Macapagal was launched.

Under the Decontrol Program, the **import control system** which was installed in the '50s was dismantled and the peso was devalued. The dismantlement of controls meant that anyone with pesos could approach his bank and apply for dollars needed to import anything -- including basketball players and fighting cocks. Goods whose importation had been banned during the time of controls to protect domestic industries, were allowed entry provided the tariffs on them were paid.

However, agricultural products remained banned.

As mentioned earlier, the *Decontrol Program* introduced us not only to devaluation but to a form of import liberalization called *tarrification*... By that, tariffs, which are decidedly a less effective method than import and foreign currency controls to protect domestic industries from foreign goods, replaced the system of controls that had been in force during the '50s.

THIRD, policies that came with the import liberalization program. This program came with the Aquino government and that program triggered the process of our return to the absolute free trade regime of the colonial period and the Bell Trade Act of 1946. Meaning, **unlimited imports free of tariff and any form of import restrictions.**

The immediate goal of this program, which started with the Aquino government, was to **dismantle** the system of **selective import controls** which Marcos had imposed during martial law in order to protect certain categories of local industries from imports. **Selective import controls represented a significant deviation from the** *Decontrol Program of 1962* **under which one could import anything,** except **agricultural goods, provided he paid the tariff.**

The *import liberalization program* started the process of dismantling both the *selective import control* and the *protective tariff system* in force during martial law.

The program would eventually culminate in our hasty accession to Gatt and membership in the WTO under the administration of Fidel V. Ramos as well as in the infamous *accelerated tariff reduction program* under which we dismantled our tariff levels at a faster pace than our trading partners agreed to do. Those tariff levels are now down to almost zero while our neighbors maintain tariff levels as high as 50 percent and even more.

FOURTH, through policies required by our **membership in Gatt, the WTO and participation in regional free trade agreements.** All these committed the Philippines, as a matter of international obligation, to the eventual goal of absolute free trade: Meaning, unrestricted imports free of tariffs and any form of controls as provided by the Bell Trade Act of 1946.

The Constitutional provision expressly limiting industrialization to industries based on agriculture

FIFTH, through Art. XII, Sec. 1, par. 2 of the Constitution which expressly limits the country's industrialization to industries based on agriculture.

THIS IS THE REALLY MORTAL FACTOR WHICH GUARANTEES THAT THE PHILIPPINES SHALL NEVER TRANSFORM INTO AN INDUSTRIAL STATE AND GRADUATE TO NIC (NEWLY INDUSTRIALIZED COUNTRY) STATUS.

That constitutional provision reads in full as follows:

> The State shall promote industrialization and full employment based on sound agricultural development and agrarian reform through industries that make full and efficient use of human and natural resources, and which are competitive in both domestic and foreign markets. However, the State shall protect Filipino enterprises against unfair foreign competition and trade practices.

Under the constitution, therefore, if the State should attempt to promote industrialization through means other than on the basis of agricultural development and agrarian reform– such as the kind of industrialization that has made NICs of our Asian neighbors, namely on the basis of metal and machine power– that kind of industrialization will be considered unconstitutional.

Q. Who in the Constitutional Commission were responsible for the Article X11, Sec. 1, par. 2?

A. That article was drafted by the Committee on the Economy and National Patrimony headed by Dr. Bernardo Villegas of the Opus Dei and personalities identified with the Makati business community.

Q. What kind of industries did the constitutional provision contemplate?

A. Apparently, industries like furniture and carpentry, rice milling, making fertilizer out of animal waste, tree planting, all forms of handicraft, food canning and the like rather than industries based on steel, metal and machine power. No engineering or machine tool and metal industry because such industries have no connection whatsoever with agriculture and land reform.

It has been through the programs and policies cited above that the U.S.– acting through the presidents whose election it has maneuvered– has managed since 1946 to prevent the industrialization of this country, apparently in obedience to the objectives laid down by the *Dodds Report* of 1946.

Q. And it all started with the *Bell Trade Act of 1946?*

A. U.S neocolonialism started with Bell Trade Act of 1946. The impositions of that Act– which we couldn't resist because they were conditions necessary for our receipt of desperately need post-war economic assistance– were what created the Philippines as America's neocolony.

Q. Please explain the *Bell Trade Act* and the circumstances under which we accepted its impositions.

THE BELL TRADE ACT OF 1946:
The start of U.S. neocolonialism and the
making of the Philippines as a neocolony.

A. The Bell Trade Act was the U.S. legislation which laid down the conditions under which the U.S. was to compensate the Philippines for damages wrought by three years of Japanese occupation.

Those conditions were: (1) extend the free trade relation that existed between the two countries during the colonial period; (2) the Philippines shall not control or regulate transactions which involve the use of dollars or foreign currency– such as for import, travel, remittances abroad by foreign companies doing business in the Philippines of their profits and capital– except upon prior approval of the President of the United States; (3) amend the Philippine Constitution so as to exempt U.S. citizens form the constitutional provision limiting the right to exploit the nation's natural resources and operate public utilities to Filipinos. This was known as the parity rights and the required amendment was known as the parity amendment; and (4) the Philippines shall not alter the peso-dollar rate of P2:P1 without the prior consent of the U.S. president.

The impositions, or conditionalities, of the Bell Act represented the destruction of the economic sovereignty that was supposed to have come with independence.

Under those impositions, the Philippines was forced by dire economic necessity to abdicate its sovereign right to do the following:

(1) protect its domestic market and domestic industries from the unlimited invasion of imports; (2) conserve
its assets of dollars and other forms of foreign currencies
through the application of controls over transactions involving the use of those currencies; (3) reserve control of
the nation's patrimony to Filipinos; and (4) change the
value of the peso in terms of foreign currencies.

The *Bell Act* in brief opened the Philippine economy
to plunder. The provision that our government couldn't
control transactions which required the use of dollars, such
as for imports, travel, overseas investment and the like,
was a clear invitation to the plunder of the nation's scarce
but valuable assets of dollars and foreign currencies.

Q. Why then did the Philippines accede to the conditions
imposed by the Bell Act?

A. Because of sheer economic necessity. We had just emerged
from three years of enemy occupation and the indescrib-
able destruction which that occupation wrought. The late
Claro M. Recto explained it in a way which caught the essence of our condition then. As he described it:

> Our country was in ruins, the national economy was com-
> pletely dislocated, there was no food, nor shelter, nor
> clothing, for our people as a result of the war. Considering
> our state of economic distress... the proponents of the Trade
> Agreement wielded a formidable weapon over our people.
> (speech on "Our Trade-Relations with the United States,"
> delivered at the Commencement Exercises of the Univer-
> sity of the East, April 5, 1954).

It was a case of plain economic blackmail applied by
the U.S. government on the very country which had proved
to be a true ally in the last world war. We stood by America's
side in that war and was dragged into it because of our status as a colony of the U.S. harboring its military and naval
bases. And for standing by the U.S. then, we suffered im-

measurable casualty and the destruction of our economy. Sensing our desperation, the U.S. government crafted a postwar rehabilitation and assistance program on condition that we remain its economic colony.

Q. What happened after passage of the *Bell Trade Act*?

A. Within three years from our acceptance of the *Bell Act* in 1946, the country had grounded to a halt. All the dollars we had received by way of rehabilitation assistance from the U.S. under the Act had evaporated by 1949, squandered on imports of non-essentials, travel and capital flight which our government was powerless to control or restrain.

Huk rebellion.-

The Bell Trade Act also served to precipitate the Communist rebellion of the '40s, and at its height that rebellion saw the Communists knocking at the doorsteps of Metro Manila.

The Philippines by 1949 was in a state of total bankruptcy.

Finding of an IMF team in 1950 that free trade had prevented the development of local industries

Mission after mission of international experts was dispatched to Manila to evaluate our crisis. One of those teams was from the IMF. In 1950, the IMF team submitted its finding to the IMF executive board and this was what that report said:

> The Bell Trade Act under which the Philippines and the United States admit each other's goods duty free had the effect of discouraging the establishment of local Philippine industries and has thereby contributed to the tendency of the Philippines to over import. (Cited in Shirley Jenkins, *U.S. Economic Policy Toward the Philippines*, Stanford University Press, 1954)

Q. Faced by the crisis and the finding of the IMF that the crisis was due to free trade provision of the Bell Trade Act, what did we do?

Brief interruption of free trade:
Protectionism and start of
industrialization in the '50s.

Protectionism and industrialization
through the installation of import and
foreign currency controls.-

A. As earlier mentioned, our government in 1950 installed a system of import and foreign exchange (currency) controls or **Forex** under which all transactions involving the use of dollars or foreign currency were subjected to Central Bank control.

Under that system, dollars were made available only for imports classified by the Central Bank as essential and necessary. Import of goods classified as non-essentials or luxuries were either subjected to quantitative limits or simply banned. The system in turn induced capitalists, both local and foreign, to invest in industries producing goods that were either banned or subject to quantitative limits. That was how industrialization started. The import control system automatically functioned to protect domestic industries from imports which in turn served as the most effective inducement for capitalists to shift their investment capital from trade and services and even agriculture to manufacturing industries producing goods that substituted for imports.

The immediate purpose of controls was to conserve the nation's dollars, which were earned chiefly from exports. We had no overseas workers then. But in time the system was developed deliberately as a policy weapon not only to conserve dollars but to foster the industrialization of the economy.

Under the system, all dollar earnings from exports and other sources had to be surrendered to the Central Bank at the official peso-dollar rate of P2:$1 and those dollars in turn were made available only to parties who would use those dollars for purposes that had to do with economic development and essential needs.

Foreign firms doing business in the Philippines couldn't convert their profits to dollars and ship those dollars out of the country any time they pleased, or even pull out their capital any time they pleased. They were required to reinvest much of their profits, and they could pull out their capital from the country only according to a timetable approved by the Central Bank.

Q. In your *Overview* you said that the World Bank in 1957 issued a report finding that the Philippines was the best performing Third World economy in the Far East, and rated only "second to Japan." Was our performance then related to the system of controls that you say was installed in 1950?

A. Definitely. Because of controls, we developed a manufacturing sector overnight and that sector was growing at the rate of 14 percent a year. That performance in turn accounted for our overall economic (GDP) growth of 7 percent a year, as the glowing World Bank report on our performance in the '50s noted.

Before 1950, our manufacturing sector accounted for a bare 8.1 percent of the economy. But by the end of that decade, the sector had grown to almost 18 percent of the economy.

Dr. Benito Legarda, Jr., former head of the Research Department of the Central Bank, noted in an article he wrote for the *Philippine Economic Journal* in 1962:

> Between 1949 and 1960 income originated in manufac-
> turing grew at the rate of 29 % a year. Relatively, it moved
> faster than other sectors *accounting for only 8.1 % in 1949
> and rising to 17.7 % in 1960.*

In his article, Dr. Legarda gives the reason for the rapid
growth of the manufacturing sector as follows:

> Quantitative restrictions acted as a protective wall be-
> hind which domestic industrialization could commence...
> The growth of manufacturing was therefore rapid.

Economic nationalism and the
Filipino First policy of Carlos P. Garcia.-

Q. What else did the system of controls accomplish?

A. Under the administration of Carlos P. Garcia, controls
was utilized not only as a policy weapon with which to induce industrialization but as a policy weapon with which
to place Filipinos in control of the economy.

Since the allocation of dollars left much to the discre-
tion of the Central Bank, it placed the government in a
position to discriminate against foreign industrialists in favor of Filipino entrepreneurs, and this was what the Central
Bank did as a matter of policy. That came to be known as
the *Filipino First* policy.

The objective of *Filipino First* was to make sure that the
growing industrialization of the economy worked to ben-
efit Filipinos first and primarily. Without *Filipino First* the
country could have been industrialized, but that industrialization would have been under the direction and control of
foreign capital.

Q. Was that the reason why the CIA decided to replace
him with Diosdado Macapagal in the elections of '61?

A. Apparently that was the reason, although the reason given was that his government was corrupt.

Corruption and controls.-

Q. But doesn't the system of controls bring about corruption– as it actually did during the '50s– and should therefore be avoided?

A. Any system of controls brings about corruption. Even a system of taxation brings about corruption. The very institution of government itself brings about corruption. But no one in his right mind would ask for the abolition of government on grounds that by its very nature it breeds corruption.

Elimination of controls:
The Decontrol Program of 1962

Q. What happened to controls?

A. In January 1962 the system of controls was dismantled by the administration of Diosdado Macapagal following the latter's election in 1961. It was in that election that we saw a then incumbent and sitting president, Carlos P. Garcia, unseated from power by an opposition party working hand in hand with the Central Intelligence Agency. (Please refer to earlier discussion on the unseating of Philippine Presidents by the CIA).

Macapagal ran for the presidency in the elections of 1961 on the pledge that he would eliminate controls and return the country to free enterprise– meaning, the role of the State in the economy shall be kept at a bare minimum, if not erased altogether, and that called for the elimination of the very system of import-foreign currency controls that had made the beginning of Philippine industrialization possible.

The Decontrol Program of 1962 constituted a step backward toward the free trade regime imposed by the Bell Trade Act of 1946.

Impact of '62 Decontrol on the economy

Q. Please summarize the impact of the Decontrol Program of 1962 on the economy.

A. I shall do that by citing no less than the National Economic Council (NEC)– which eventually was renamed NEDA– on the impact of the Decontrol Program of '62 on the economy:

> Industry (manufacturing) was subjected to severe repressive conditions during the period 1962 to 1965. The effect of decontrol which increased the capital and operating requirements of industries on one hand, coupled with the tight credit policy instituted by the government, on the other, resulted in tight squeeze greatly prejudicial to industrial enterprises. The growth of technical smuggling together with massive importation of consumer goods dumped from abroad subjected local industrial enterprises to severe competition resulting to reduced sales volume and reduced prices of local manufactured goods. . .
>
> *The figures indicate that industry operating under the inertia of the pre-decontrol period was able to withstand the transitional difficulties initially, but finally bent over in 1965 when the output of the manufacturing sector increased by only less than one percent.* (Statistical Reporter, Office of Statistical Coordination and Standards, National Economic Council, Vol. X111, No. 2 issue of April-June 1969).

When Marcos assumed the presidency in 1966, he reported to Congress that there were more than 1000 industries facing closure.

U.S. pressure in the late '50s to have
controls dismantled and the peso devalued.-

Q. What did the U.S. have to say about the Decontrol Program of 1962?

A. The U.S. wanted just that and to facilitate the program the U.S. and the IMF, on Macapagal's election, approved immediately a stabilization loan of $300 million to the Macapagal administration on the pledge that it would dismantle the system of controls and devalue the peso, which it did.

In fact during the Garcia administration, the U.S. had begun exerting pressure on the Central Bank to dismantle controls and devalue the peso. As early as then, the U.S. wanted the Philippines to return to free trade. When then CB Governor Miguel Cuaderno applied to the IMF for a stabilization loan of $25 million, the U.S. State Department pressured the IMF to deny the Philippine application unless our Central Bank dismantled controls and devalued. CB Governor Cuaderno resisted the pressure and returned to Manila without the $25 million stabilization loan.

Q. How do you know that?

A. CB Governor Cuaderno recounted the incident in an autobiographical work that he wrote after his retirement from public service. This was what he said about that incident in his book *Problems of Economic Development:*

> I felt very deeply the refusal of (IMF) Managing Director Per Jacobson to have his staff discuss our stabilization program with our mission *when he learned that the State Department did not favor it.* I thought it was not good policy for an international organization such as the International Monetary Fund to allow itself to be influenced by any member country.

> We had a feeling that what the U.S. Government officials liked us to do was to devalue the peso and remove exchange controls. Such a step has been suggested to us by both the Managing Director of the Fund and some officials of the State Department.

Q. You say that as far back as 1950, the IMF had acknowledged that free trade resulted in *"discouraging the establishment of local Philippine industries."*,

A. Yes.

Q. Why then does the IMF insist through its conditionalities that the Philippines open up to imports as widely as possible and return to free trade?

A. Presumably because of the **Dodds Report** and U.S. interventionism in the affairs and decisions of the IMF.

Under the IMF conditionalities no country with a preindustrial economy can possibly industrialize and become an NIC. That explains the poverty, the technological backwardness and now the hunger.

Q. Please summarize what the IMF conditionalities amount to and why they have worked to prevent this country from industrializing.

A. The IMF conditionalities amount to four commands: (1) Keep the economy open to imports and foreign investments as widely as possible– meaning, no tariffs, or if tariffs can't be avoided, those tariffs should be kept as low as possible and, above all, no import controls; (2) maintain a foreign exchange policy "free from restrictions,"– meaning no control over transactions involving the use of dollars or foreign currency, such as for import, foreign travel and investments overseas; (3) keep devaluating the peso; and (4) follow a policy of fiscal and monetary austerity– meaning, be austere with welfare projects and the social services and maintain a high interest rate policy.

Those four commands are tantamount to economic suicide through slow hunger – which is what we are experiencing now. With these conditions, a nation which has yet to see the glimmer of an industrial revolution simply starves.

Q. Is it your thesis that our governments have been yielding to those conditionalities since 1962 because that's what the U.S. has instructed our presidents who owe their election to the CIA?

A. That's part of the answer. And obviously that's what former President Diosdado Macapagal meant when he wrote his article in the *Bulletin* urging the Philippines to be truly independent- obviously of the U.S.- so that this country can "hasten its becoming an NIC" and eliminate poverty.

He knew what he was talking about.

Q. What's the other part of the answer?

The rise of a class of economic officials, known as technocrats, who, since 1966, have functioned as executors of the anti-industrialization plan of the *Dodds Report* and the conditionalities of the IMF-WB Group.

A. The other part of the answer is that since the mid-sixties, beginning with the Marcos administration, there emerged and developed a class of economic functionaries who serve as virtual proxies of the IMF and the World Bank. These functionaries, known as **technocrats**, have been put in charge of sensitive policy-making and policy-implementing bodies and over the years they have come to dictate the economic policies of the nation.

Q. When you say that these technocrats have been the virtual proxies of the IMF what do you mean?

A. I mean that they echo the economic ideology as well as the policies which those two institutions ask our governments to adopt in exchange for foreign loans – which those technocrats themselves urge our government to seek from the IMF.

In brief, it is principally through the technocrats that the IMF and WB have pushed this country to those programs and policies that have blocked the industrialization of the economy and prevented the Philippines from joining the ranks of Asian NICs.

So that between Philippine presidents elected through U.S. interventionism, on one hand, and technocrats who echo what the U.S.– IMF-WB Group tells the Philippines should do, on the other hand, this country has had no way of framing an independent economic program that could have transformed the Philippines into an industrial state.

Q. Please summarize the essential elements of the economic thinking of the technocrats.

Main elements of the economic ideology of the *technocrats*

A. Technocrats believe in, and have vigorously pushed for, the following: (1) an economy open as much as possible to imports, which means minimal or virtual absence of tariffs and import controls with which to protect local industries; (2) a policy encouraging the peso to devalue in order to make Philippine exports attractive to foreign buyers.

In addition, the technocrats have consistently opposed the idea of an industrialization based on the heavy industries, such as steel, engine and machine production, machine tools, petrochemicals, and the like. At most, they would concede to an industrialization based on agriculture and light industries that are labor intensive, such as furniture making, rice milling and canning of agricultural products– *but never to an industrialization based on machine power and which produce what are called the means of production, which constitute the core of any industrialization program.*

When Ferdinand Marcos decided in 1979 to launch an industrialization program based on the steel, machine and heavy industries, his own technocrats joined the IMF and the WB in resisting the program and insisted on its indefinite deferment.

No president after Marcos made any move to transform the Philippines into an NIC. No economic program following Edsa ever contemplated a plan for developing the capital goods industry which is indispensable to real industrialization.

IN FACT, THE PRESENT CONSTITUTION IN-CLUDES A SPECIFIC PROVISION THAT LIMITS ANY INDUSTRIALIZATION PROGRAM TO ONE THAT IS BASED ON *"SOUND AGRICULTURAL DEVELOPMENT AND AGRARIAN REFORM."*

Through the cited constitutional provision, elements who had opposed the major industrial projects of Marcos– ranking members of the Makati business community and the Church-based Opus Dei– made sure that no president or government after Marcos ever attempt to promote the heavy industries in this country because to do so would be unconstitutional.

Q. What proof do you have that Marcos technocrats opposed Marcos's plan for industrialization?

A. That's a matter of public record, and Marcos himself is on record that his own technocrats had opposed his industrialization plan.

Q. Would you cite such instances?

A. American scholar Robin Broad has given a detailed account of how the IMF and the World Bank and then Prime Minister Cesar Virata blocked Marcos' industrialization projects from the start.

An international affairs fellow of the Council on Foreign Relations, Broad writes this revealing inside account in her book *Unequal Alliance:*

> In December 1979, only a couple of months after the Philippine government had inaugurated the idea of the eleven projects with great fanfare, Minister Ongpin stood before the World Bank-led Consultative Group to explain away the doubts (about the projects)...

> Continued remonstrances by the World Bank and the IMF against the eleven projects necessitated further capitulation...Although the World Bank approved Ongpin's two new caveats as far as some of the projects were concerned, it was exerting heavy pressure on the Philippines to scuttle the steel mill and the petrochemical projects – both in the view of nationalists– critical for autonomous Philippine industrialization.

She then proceeds to reveal how Virata supported the IMF-WB position against the projects by voicing the opinion that some of the projects were not viable.

> Thus although Ongpin's rhetoric remained firm, by 1981– almost halfway through the original implementation timetable for the completion of the eleven– *Minister Virata was able to voice his forebodings that feasibility studies would disclose some of the projects not to be viable.*

But as Broad devastatingly revealed:

> *Conveniently ignored were earlier documents and an-*
> *nouncements on the major industrial projects that had cited*
> *completed, favorable feasibility studies for the whole group.*

Q. You say that Marcos lashed out against his own technocrats and accused them of colluding with the industrial powers to prevent the industrialization of the country. When did he do that and who were the technocrats do you think he had in mind.

A. Marcos lashed out against his own technocrats in 1982 when he accused his critics– which then included his own technocrats led by Virata and BOI chairman Vicente T. Paterno– as **"all part of a plot to insure that this country remains under the industrial countries."** (see story "Marcos hits critics of major projects," *Times Journal, May 24, 1982).*

The crucial role of the BOI under Vicente T. Paterno
in blocking the industrialization program of Marcos
and the high honor given Paterno
by the Japanese government.-

Paterno, who served as BOI chairman throughout the decade of the '70s was perhaps in the best position among all the technocrats to implement an industrial program. But the first thing he did when Marcos declared martial law was to **delist** heavy industries, like steel and petrochemicals, from the investment priorities of the government. That was about the time that Park Chung-hee of South Korea decided that he would establish an integrated steel mill and an engine industry.

Then, in 1982, as a member of the *Batasan* (the Congress during Martial Law years) Paterno made the surprising statement:

> Spending $1.2 billion in an integrated steel mill almost seems *criminal* because the project won't answer the chief need of the economy at this time. (story titled "Paterno calls 11 projects untimely," *Times Journal,* Sept. 26, 1982.)

But an even more revealing statement of Paterno – which explains why the Philippines never industrialized under his long tenure as BOI chairman – was his confession that *"Even as minister of industry he had held that 'industry should take a back seat to agriculture.'"* (see "Paterno says agriculture should take priority over industry." *Business Day,* October 7, 1982)

Following his resignation as BOI chairman, the Japanese government invested Paterno with "one of the highest honors" that the Japanese government can give a foreign citizen.

Q. How do you know that?

A. From a story which appeared in the *Financial Times* (Manila) in the November 27, 1981 issue of that paper. I quote a paragraph in that story, which was titled "**Paterno conferred major award by Tokyo gov't.**"

> On the official representation of Japanese industrialists, the Tokyo government has conferred upon the former cabinet official of President Marcos the award of first class order of the sacred treasure for his role in promoting strong economic relations between the Philippines during his incumbency in office.

Significantly, Marcos leveled his accusation after earlier complaining publicly that: "**We got caught with what the technocrats were saying every time, that it was not the best of times and so they kept postponing and postponing it.**" (*Times Journal,* Jan. 31, 1982).

Decidedly, Paterno was among the technocrats Marcos was alluding to when he complained in public that "they kept postponing and postponing it (the industrial project).

Q. Was there opposition in the private sector against the 11 major industrial projects of Marcos?

A. In the private sector opposition to the industrial projects came chiefly from ranking members of the Makati business community and the Opus Dei.

Prominent in the opposition was Dr. Bernardo Villegas of the Opus Dei. Villegas openly supported the position of the IMF and WB that the industrial projects should be deferred – meaning, shelved indefinitely, and it has remained shelved to this day.

Q. And how about the technocrats who came with governments after Marcos?

Technocrats in the post-Marcos era:
The Aquino technocrats accused of economic treason
in the Senate and as "slaves of the IMF."

It was during the Aquino administration that the government started its plunge into that policy mix of import liberalization and devaluation with hardly any letup. The drive toward that deadly policy mix was spearheaded by NEDA and the policy was implemented by the Central Bank and the Finance Department.

Except for former Trade and Industry Minister Jose Concepcion, Jr., who served the Aquino administration, I can't name any technocrat who came with governments after Marcos who proposed a program of industrialization. All--except for Concepcion and to a certain extent former House Speaker Ramon V. Mitra who served as Agricultrue Secretary under Aquino-- were pushing for import liberalization, free trade and devaluation at breakneck speed.

In fact, two of the Aquino technocrats, Dr. Jesus Estanislao and Jose Cuisia, Jr., who served as Finance Secretary and Central Bank governor, respectively, were accused by DTI Secretary Concepcion of being "slaves of the IMF," and in the Senate they were accused of "consummated treason."

Q. On what occasion did DTI Secretary Concepcion accuse CB Governor Cuisia and Finance Secretary Estanislao of being "slaves of the IMF"?

A. Concepcion hurled his accusation at his two colleagues in the Aquino cabinet before the Weekly Congress Forum on December 28,1990. In that forum Concepcion assailed the two for their docility in dealing with the IMF and for bowing down to IMF demands that the import liberalization program be pushed through.

In that speech, Concepcion revealed that **"the import liberalization policy has displaced 700,000 workers and killed small local industries."**

The Concepcion speech was reported by the *Philippine Daily Globe* in that paper's issue of December 29, 1990 in a story titled "JoeCon hits cabinet for bowing to IMF– chides cabinet members for being slaves of the IMF."

Q. On what occasion were Cuisia and Estanislao accused of economic treason in the Senate?

A. The occasion was provoked by the refusal of Cuisia and Estanislao to reveal the terms of the agreement they had reached with the IMF.

Q. Who were the senators who accused Cuisia and Estanislao of economic treason?

A. Then Senators Joseph Estrada, Teofisto Guingona, Aquilino Pimentel and Alberto Romulo.

According to a story of the incident carried by the *Philippine Daily Globe* issue of February 4, 1991 titled "Solons want Cuisia, Estanislao arrested:"

Irate senators will seek the arrest of Finance Secretary Jesus Estanislao and Central Bank designate Jose Cuisia on charges of alleged 'consummated treason' for selling the country to foreign creditors...

Senator Estrada is set to ask the Department of Justice to cause the immediate arrest of Estanislao and Cuisia upon return from abroad where they concluded negotiations with the International Monetary Fund (IMF).

Estrada and Senate Majority Floor Leader Guingona, Jr., earlier demanded sanctions against the two debt negotiators for allegedly conspiring with the IMF at the expense of the Filipino people.

A consistent debt relief advocate (Sen. Alberto) Romulo said that apart from charging Estanislao and Cuisia with treason, 'Congress should now pass laws revoking authority from the debt negotiators to do what they are doing.

The Ramos administration and the Asian crisis of 1997-

Q. What about governments after Aquino?

A. We can begin with the administration of Fidel V. Ramos, which succeeded the Aquino administration. We know that it was the Ramos administration which pushed the country headlong into GATT, the WTO and globalization– with hardly any safety nets. Just like jumping from the top of the Empire State Building without safety nets.

In the latter part of his term, Ramos pushed his **accelerated tariff reduction program** under which the Philippine government unilaterally reduced the country's tariff levels at a faster pace than the country's Asean partners did. That put the Philippines, of course, at a great disadvantage vis-à-vis the neighbors.

In military parlance, it was as if the nation unilaterally disarmed while the adversaries maintained their defenses.

Our partners now have higher tariff levels than what we maintain. That's why foreign manufacturers here prefer to locate their plants in countries like Vietnam and Thailand because those countries provide a higher level of protection for their industries than the Philippines does.

Liberalization of financial system and rules on foreign currency transactions. –

Ramos technocrats also completely liberalized the nation's policy on foreign currency transactions to achieve the ideal of a "foreign exchange system free of restrictions," so greatly desired by the IMF. It was on account of that reckless liberalization that we were fully exposed to the destabilizing movements of speculative capital, or what is known as "hot money," and it was that which made the economy vulnerable to the Asian crisis of 1997. The unrestricted movement of foreign speculative capital during and following that year caused the eventual devaluation of the peso from its pre-crisis level of P26:$1 to its present level of P56:$1.

When the technocrats of Fidel V. Ramos totally liberalized the nation's rules on foreign currency transactions, they provided speculative foreign capital, or what is known as "hot money," complete freedom to move in and out of the country at will. Most of that came into the country to gamble in our stock market.

And so when financial panic hit the region following the financial crisis in Thailand, the speculative capital that foreigners had put into the stock market pulled out of this country *en masse* and our government couldn't restrain that pullout precisely because it had committed never to interfere with the movement of foreign capital. That was a major reason for the devaluation of the peso.

There was another lunatic aspect to the policy. Under that policy, anyone– Filipino and foreigner alike– could borrow pesos from his bank and use those pesos to purchase dollars which were then either hoarded or moved out of the country. That was known as "selling the peso short."

The peso borrowed from the bank was eventually repaid after the dollar value of the peso had gone down. For example, speculators borrowed pesos to buy dollars at, say, P26:$1. So, with P26 million one could buy $1 million.

They then held on to those dollars until the peso-rate had shot up to P40:$1. At that point, they sold their dollars for pesos to repay the loan– with resulting profit because the one million dollars acquired at a cost of P26 million could then be sold for P40 million.

The effect of that was to drive down the value of the peso– which meant devaluation. That was another reason why the peso-dollar rate soared from the pre-crisis level of P26:$1 to its present rate of P56:$1.

Q. But what should our government have done?

A. First, the Ramos government should never have completely liberalized the nation's rules on foreign currency transactions. We should never have allowed foreign investors, particularly foreign stock and money speculators, to come in and out of the country as they please.

Second, when the Asian crisis struck and foreign speculators started moving out their dollars from the country, our government should have done what Malaysia's Mahathir did. Mahathir moved swiftly to prevent foreign currency from moving out of Malaysia at will. He imposed foreign currency controls in defiance of IMF-WB wishes. In brief, he struck down the freedom of foreign investors to take their capital out of Malaysia anytime they pleased, and by that he managed to conserve the integrity and stability of the Malaysian currency. A foreign investor in Malaysia's stock market, for example, just couldn't sell his Malaysian stocks and with the proceeds buy dollars to be shipped out of Malaysia.

Mahathir froze billions of dollars of foreign speculative and investment capital in Malaysia and prohibited them from moving out of his country.

Q. But didn't every country in the region do what Ramos did– which was to lift all restrictions on transactions involving foreign currency completely, that is, liberalized rules on foreign currency transactions?

A. Certainly not. The countries who refused to liberalize their rules on foreign currency transactions were Taiwan, China, India and Vietnam. That's why these countries were spared from what has been called the "Asian flu" which struck the region in 1997 and which caused the radical devaluation of Asian currencies, including the peso.

**Taiwan Central Bank describes as "reckless"
the action of Asian governments, like the Philippines,
in lifting restrictions on foreign currency transactions
and liberalizing the financial system**

In fact, when the London-based *Economist* (issue of April 25, 1998) interviewed the head of the Central Bank of Taiwan on how Taiwan managed to escape the Asian crisis, the answer simply was that "**other Asian countries** – (obviously referring, among others, to the Philippines)– **liberalized their financial systems** *recklessly*."

Here is the passage of that article on Taiwan and the accusation of "recklessness" which the Taiwan Central Bank leveled at other Asian governments, such as the Philippines:

> Taiwan has escaped largely unscathed by Asian financial crisis…The lesson drawn by Taiwan's central bank, the Central Bank of China (CBC) is that *other Asian countries liberalized their financial systems recklessly.*

Q. Were there foreign parties other than Taiwan which believed that the liberalization of the nation's financial system was a mistake?

ADB advises India and China
not to follow Philippine example
in opening their economies hastily

A. There was, and that was no less than the Asian Development Bank (ADB) itself.

I quote from a *Reuters* dispatch, published in the business section of *Today* in that paper's issue of March 21, 2000. The story was titled "India, China told to go slow."

> The Asian Development Bank said on Friday that China, India, Vietnam and Pakistan were vulnerable to a financial crisis of a kind that swept other parts of Asia in 1997 and 1998 if they opened up their economies hastily.

The warning issued by the ADB was clearly a way of criticizing the "recklessness" and haste with which countries like the Philippines liberalized their economies and financial system.

In referring specifically to Indonesia, Thailand, Malaysia and the Philippines, the ADB said that "**The root causes of the crisis of confidence were not weak macroeconomic fundamentals but structural problems** *including liberalization of financial markets without adequate supervision…*"

Q. And Ramos liberalized our foreign control rules in consultation with his technocrats?

A. One must assume so.

Q. And after Ramos?

A. After Ramos came Estrada. Estrada assumed the presidency fully aware that the U.S. had undermined the 11 major industrial projects of Marcos. He said as much in an interview with *Asiaweek* soon after the elections of 1998.

But Estrada never took the effort to restore Marcos's industrial projects. Instead, he continued with the globalization and free trade legacy bequeathed to him by the Ramos administration. He likewise surrounded himself with technocrats who were adherents of free trade and globalization.

Early on in his presidency, Estrada launched a drive to eliminate the nationalist provisions in the Constitution which reserve the right to land ownership and the nation's patrimony to citizens of the Philippines. He set about to de-Filipinize and globalize the Constitution as what his predecessor Fidel V. Ramos tried to do.

The administration of Estrada was rocked by the divisive national debate provoked by his move to de-Filipinize the Constitution and his political downfall started with that.

One must also recall here that when the nationalist Mahathir of Malaysia had his Deputy Prime Minister Anwar Ibrahim arrested for allegedly undermining Malaysia's national interest by colluding with the IMF and the WB—agencies which Mahathir described as the *agents of the new colonialism* – Estrada joined the U.S. and Western financial community in taking side with Anwar.

As a reputed Filipino nationalist, Estrada should have taken the side of Mahathir, but he didn't and instead took the side of Anwar, the globalist.

The issue arose in the wake of the Asian crisis, and Mahathir's response to that crisis was to impose foreign currency controls, to which the IMF-WB and the Western powers led by the U.S. objected. Anwar took the side of the IMF-WB.

The Mahathir-Anwar issue represented a frontal collision between nationalist and globalist forces in Malaysia, and Estrada joined the community of globalists in ganging up on Mahathir instead of taking pain to understand what Mahathir stood for.

Following his visit to Malaysia, Estrada pledged that he wouldn't do what Mahathir did and that his, Estrada's, administration would stick to the IMF-WB prescription of refraining from any controls on foreign currency transactions.

In the end Mahathir has been vindicated by events. His solution to Malaysia's problem when the Asian crisis struck– which was to institute foreign currency controls and peg the Malaysian currency to a fixed rate of exchange in violation of IMF-WB commandments– proved to have been the correct one although universally denounced at the time by the U.S. and the Western powers, including the Philippines.

Q. And Gloria Macapagal-Arroyo?

A. We know that it was Gloria Macapagal-Arroyo as chair of the senate committee on economic affairs in 1994 who steered the senate into a hasty ratification of GATT. To her credit, however, after assuming the presidency she did take steps to restrain the momentum toward absolute free trade which the administration of Fidel V. Ramos had set in motion. She gave instructions to restrain what she called "unbridled globalization" but hers were half-hearted steps which hardly measured up to the problems and which simply dramatize her disastrous misjudgment in steering the

Senate into recklessly ratifying GATT during her tenure as chair of the senate committee on economic affairs.

Macapagal-Arroyo could and should have learned from the disastrous experience of her father who launched the Decontrol Program in 1962 and paid the political cost of the economic error of that program.

At least, when Diosdado Macapagal eliminated foreign currency and import controls, he installed a system of protective tariffs to cushion the impact of import de-regulation. But Macapagal-Arroyo went even as far as to commit the nation to an international agreement designed to eliminate tariffs altogether. Under her watch, the Philippines is now scheduled to return to the regime of absolute free trade that prevailed during the colonial period.

The technocrats she appointed, the latest of whom at this time of writing is Romulo Neri of NEDA, are globalists and– if one may repeat and stress this– not a single one has ever been heard to talk of or even mention industrialization or the need to develop the capital goods industry which holds the key to industrialization.

One should ask Neri and company to explain how they propose to follow in the footsteps of the Asian NICs and whether they have any program at all for developing the *capital goods* industry, without which industrialization is impossible.

In sum, the defining characteristic of the technocrats has been their fierce and unrelenting opposition to economic protectionism, their hostility to an industrialization based on machine power or the so-called heavy industries, and a mindset which looks at globalization and free trade as realities whose decrees simply have to be followed, even if to do so spells the literal collapse of the economy.

That's why technocrats have functioned as the ideal agents for implementing, as they have done, the anti-industrialization objective of the *Dodds Report* and the free trade conditionalities of the IMF.

It has been under the economic governance of the technocrats that– if one may recall the ominous article of Ceferino Follosco "A scheme to destroy industries"– the entire industrial infrastructure developed during the '50s, which made the Philippines the preeminent economy in the Asia Pacific during that decade, was dismantled.

Under their economic governance, this country witnessed the death of the National Steel Corporation, which used to be the largest producer of steel products in the Asean.

The world has yet to see another example of a sovereign nation-state allowing such a strategic industry as steel to disintegrate in the name of free trade and free market economics.

Q. But where did the technocrats learn their economics?

A. That's an important question, and that brings us to the role of schools and universities, especially U.P School of Economics, in the formulation of a post-Edsa development strategy that lent itself to the neocolonial objective of opening up markets of Third World economies and forcing the devaluation of their currencies– in brief, the mix of free trade and devaluation which has proved devastatingly fatal to this country: The mix which has given rise to the hunger and preserved the Philippines as a raw material economy, pursuant to the mandate of the *Dodds s Report*.

5

THE ROLE OF THE ACADEMIC COMMUNITY AND THE U.P. SCHOOL OF ECONOMICS IN THE MAKING OF THE *PHILIPPINE CRISIS*

Starting in the '60s the U.P School of Economics– the nation's most prominent and prestigious school of economics– began aggressively promoting the notion that economic protectionism is bad economics and that the road to development lies in allowing "market forces" free and uninhibited play in the economy– even if that meant destroying the economy itself.

It's a philosophy based in turn on the notion that free trade and the unrestrained workings of market forces are ends in themselves which should be pursued at all cost, irrespective of social, political and economic consequences.

The five deadly policy commands of the economics taught at the U.P. School of Economics.-

In terms of specific policy advocacy the U.P. free market line translates into the following policy commands: (1) Avoidance of all and any barrier to imports of all goods, manufacturing, and agricultural, whether in the form of import and currency controls, tariffs and government support of domestic industry, such as subsidies to farmers and price support of agricultural goods; (2) industrialization should be based on labor-intensive, export-oriented or LIEO industries; (3) avoidance of industries that require an intensive investment of capital or what is known *capital-intensive* industries; and (4) non-interventionist role of the State in the economy; meaning no price controls, no involvement in any form of business activity and the like; and (5) the use of devaluation as a policy to make exports competitive.

Q. Please give examples of LIEO industries and capital-intensive industries.

A. Examples of labor-intensive, export-oriented industries or LIEO are: furniture making and the various handicrafts, production of shoes, slippers, and garments, canning of fruits and food products, including drying of seaweeds, making of wigs and the various forms of cottage industries, such as making of candles and toys– all of which don't require extensive use of investment capital but involve the intensive use of labor.

Examples of capital-intensive industries are the production of steel out of raw ore, the manufacture of engines and machines, petrochemicals, machine tool, automobile production (and not only automobile assembly), shipbuilding and the like.

Capital-intensive industries are generally referred to as the *heavy industries* and basic industries: Heavy industries because they involve the use of heavy machinery, and basic industries because they are identified with the production of *capital goods* or the *means of production.*

Q. What do you mean when you say that capital-intensive industries are industries that produce *capital goods* or the *means of production?*

A. These capital-intensive industries are the modern *means of production* –the machineries, industrial tools and equipment with which to produce or manufacture goods and provide services. You can't, for example, produce canned sardines without the use of machinery; you can't produce shirts and trousers without the use of the machinery that go into the making of a textile mill. You can't even make tables and chairs without using the tools, such as axe and hammer, produced by the machine and tool industry.

That's the reason why capital-intensive industries are regarded as basic industries: They produce the instruments and equipment basic to the production of goods. Without these capital-intensive industries, or what is also known as *capital goods industry*, man can produce goods only with his hands and feet, as they used to in ancient times before the age of the machine.

Q. Are labor intensive, export oriented industries bad?

A. No. In fact, they should be encouraged.

Q. Then what's wrong with the economics taught at the U.P if it advocates the promotion of *labor-intensive, export-oriented industries?*

A. What's wrong with the economics taught at the U.P is that: (1) it would limit the industrialization of the Philippines to the labor-intensive export-oriented industries **to the exclusion of the basic, capital-goods industries;** (2) it would make the continuous devaluation of the peso a policy instrument to encourage the export of the products of labor-intensive industries, thereby creating a ceaseless round of price increases that work, as it has worked, havoc on the already enfeebled purchasing power of the masses; and (3) through its insistence on total free trade, it hasn't only killed domestic manufacturing industries but also the nation's agricultural sector.

There is nothing wrong with pushing for the development of labor-intensive, export-oriented industries if it is pushed along with the development of the basic, heavy industries producing the modern *means of production*– the machinery, equipment, machine tools without which a country can't possibly be competitive in the international market.

But the economics they teach at the U.P., judging by the pronouncements of the products of that institution, would literally ban the development of the *capital goods* industry and no country has developed without such an industry.

Furthermore, in their advocacy of free trade, the U.P. economists have extended it to apply to the agricultural sector – resulting in the flood of agricultural imports which have virtually marginalized the nation's agricultural sector.

Q. Has the government adopted the kind of economics taught at the U.P.?

A. Yes. That's essentially the economics which the government adopted for the most part of the martial law regime and it's the economics enshrined in **Art. X11, Sec. 1, par. 2** of the Constitution which limits industrialization to industries based on "sound agricultural development and agrarian reform."

It's the deadly policy commands of the economics taught at the U.P that have dominated the development strategy of all governments that came with people power in 1986: (1) import liberalization, leading to the dismantlement of tariff and import controls; (2) continuous devaluation of the peso and privatization; and (3) monetary and fiscal austerity, which spells high interest rates and austerity in social services; and rejection of the heavy industries that made NICs of our neighbors.

All commands have resulted in de-industrialization, the marginalization of agriculture, rising joblessness coupled with rising prices, acute shortage of social services and, eventually, hunger.

Q. Since when has the U.P. brand of economics been applied by the government?

A. It started with the appointment of Dr. Gerardo Sicat to the chairmanship of the NEDA in 1970. Following people power and the retirement of Sicat from government, the U.P. brand of economics was adopted by the government through the appointment of Solita Monsod, also a product of the U.P. School of Economics as chair of NEDA. Monsod was succeeded by appointees largely recruited from the U.P. School of Economics, all of whom are avowed free traders opposed to the development of the capital goods industry or what are known as *capital-intensive* industries.

Sicat was the U.P professor most active in the promotion of the LIEO development strategy and the use of devaluation as a policy instrument to encourage exports. He may aptly be called the father of the LIEO development strategy.

Q. What makes you say that?

A. I say that on the basis of his voluminous writings while assistant professor at the U.P. School of Economics in which he assiduously pushed for the LIEO development strategy.

Those writings were collected and compiled in a book titled *Economic Policy and Philippine Development*, which was published by the University of the Philippine Press in 1972.

Q. Would you cite passages from his writings which warrant your criticism of the economic thinking which he represents?

A. For example, this is what he had to say about capital-intensive industries in his cited book *Economic Policy and Philippine Development*:

> We shall have a better set of policies if we can abolish all the incentives currently in effect by law which tend to encourage capital-use. It is desirable to make this proposal apply to all industrial activities. (p. 46)

That passage is literally a call for de-listing from the government's priority investment program all industries that are deemed "capital intensive," which was what happened soon after martial law was declared.

Sicat also revealed strong sympathy for Hong Kong as an economic model, as evident in the following passage:

> The tremendous growth of that small colony, based only on the cheap labor, liberal foreign investments attraction policy *and free trade*, is one of the growth miracles of the post- World War 11 period in Asia. . .In fact we would emphasize that there is much we can adopt from the Hong Kong experience that can be valuable to us. (p. 178).

Like free trade for example.

Q. Who funded the publication of his studies?

A. The financial support received by Sicat for most of the articles which constituted his aforementioned book came from two sources: the U.P. School of Economics and the Rockefeller Foundation.

Q. How do you know that the Rockefeller Foundation was involved in the financing of the works of Sicat?

A. He acknowledged that in the *Preface* to his book. In it he said:

Without giving them responsibility, I must thank the School of Economics of the University of the Philippines and the *Rockefeller Foundation* for *financial support* in the writing of most of these studies.

In addition to the aforesaid acknowledgement, Sicat added a word of thanks for the assistance he received from three non-Filipinos, namely, Richard Hooley, John Power, and Jeffrey Williamson.

It must be stressed, however, that the U.P. School of Economics isn't the only educational institution that has espoused or identified itself with the free trade school. "Elite" schools led by the Ateneo and De La Salle have been as guilty though not as prominently as the U.P. School of Economics in endorsing free trade economics– which, as history has abundantly established, has always served as the economic basis and ideological weapon of colonialism in keeping colonies poor.

Free trade is nothing more but the economics of colonialism and that's what the schools in this country teach, and which they implant in the minds of their students as the one and only "correct" economics.

6

THE FISCAL CRISIS

Q. Please explain the fiscal crisis.

A. It is the crisis of a government that can't raise the revenue with which to meet its expenses and declared targets. It is, analogously, the crisis of a household whose income consistently fails to meet its financial requirements and which must therefore be constantly borrowing to make both ends meet, except that this time, even its borrowings aren't sufficient to make up for the deficit. And so the household simply threatens to disintegrate. It can't pay the servants, it can't pay for the tuition of the children, it can't meet hospital bills, it can't get its car repaired, etc.

Q. Everyone says that the fiscal crisis is due to corruption. Do you agree?

A. Disagree. And I do so on the authority of former Finance Secretary Isidro Camacho who, just before he resigned from government, admitted that the accelerated tariff reduction program of the government accounts for 50 percent of the budgetary deficit.

As to the remaining 50 percent of the deficit, same is accounted for partly by the fact that businesses have been either bankrupted by the tariff reduction program or rendered less profitable by it and partly by what is known as "leakages," which, of course, means corruption.

So you can see that corruption represents only a minority factor in the range of causes that have led to the fiscal crisis.

Q. What is your authority for your statements?

Q. In its issue of October 16, 2003, the *Manila Standard* quotes Camacho to that effect. It quoted the former finance secretary in connection with a story which that paper ran reporting on the call of Senator Ralph Recto for a review of the nation's tariff laws. Recto complained that the government's tariff reduction program has caused great loss in revenue and apparently the former finance secretary agreed with Recto.

As the story put it:

> Finance Secretary Jose Isidro Camacho said foregone revenue from tariff cuts would have been enough to cut our budget deficit by half. ("Recto calls for tariff cut review").

Q. What accounts for the other half of the budgetary deficit?

A. According to a *Reuters* dispatch, which was published in the November 26, 2002 issue of the *Inquirer*, approximately a third of the budgetary deficit is accounted for by the downsizing of corporate profits. The story, titled "Taxing times for Philippines as revenues slump," quotes a financial ambassador as source. By that ambassador's count, one-third of the deficit is due to tariff reduction, one-third to the slump in business profits caused by tariff reduction and the rest, or one-third, to corruption.

Another source from Congress, aside from Senator Recto, is Rep. Herminio Teves. According to Teves, citing figures from the Tariff Commission: "from 1997 to 2002, annual tariff collections dropped by an average of 6 percent each year, from a **high** of P83 billion in 1997 to just P59.5 billion last year (2001).

As Teves significantly added:

> THIS IS NOT TO MENTION THE ECONOMIC DIFFI-
> CULTIES, INCLUDING JOB LOSSES, WE'VE SUFFERED
> AS A RESULT OF THE FLOOD OF IMPORTS THAT UN-
> DERMINE LOCAL MANUFACTURERS AND FARMERS.
> ("Past tariff cuts harmed us," *Today,* July 28, 2003).

The matter couldn't have been stated more succinctly and effectively.

In essence then, it was import liberalization and the reckless tariff reduction program of the government coupled with the bankruptcies and profit losses caused by import liberalization which must be held principally responsible for the fiscal crisis, and not corruption.

After all if giant enterprises like Hacienda Luisita, Caltex, National Steel and Matsushita Electric could be forced to either marginalize operations or close shop altogether because of imports and the tariff reduction program, what more of the tens of thousands of lesser known enterprises who could otherwise be continuing sources of revenues for the government?

The point is that the drive toward free trade, and not corruption, explains the fiscal crisis. That drive has bankrupted the economy and the bankruptcy of the economy in turn is what the fiscal crisis reflects.

The fiscal crisis is primarily the making of the technocrats and not of the corrupt tax collectors or even of corrupt taxpayers. The fiscal crisis is merely one aspect– and in fact a necessary consequence– of the *Philippine crisis,* for which the technocrats have much to account.

7

THE DEBT CRISIS AND ITS ORIGIN:
From Debt Trap to Debt Slavery,
From a Nation of Debtors
to a Nation of Slaves

Q. Would you explain the problem with the foreign debt? How exactly did the problem begin?

A. Let's take a look at the following table and trace how the foreign debt grew from a bare $150 million in 1961 to the $56 billion monstrosity that it is today.

Table 8

Foreign debt

1961	$150 Million
1965	$600 Million
2005	**$56 Billion**

The supreme tragedy, of course, is that after more than 40 years of borrowing, we have absolutely nothing to show for what we borrowed. In fact, the conditionalities attached to the loans operated, and were in fact calculated, to prevent the nation from developing into an industrial state the way the neighbors have done. Those conditionalities killed the very industries that we had managed to establish *before* the borrowings began, such as Caltex refining and National Steel Corporation, along with the tire, textile, appliance and other industries.

The debt problem began in January 1962 when the then newly elected administration of Diosdado Macapagal approached the U.S. State Department and the IMF for a stabilization loan of $300 million

Prior to 1962, our foreign debt, as you can see, stood at a bare $150 million.

The application for the loan of $300 million was made on the pledge that the Philippine government will: (1) devalue the peso and (2) lift the entire system of foreign currency and import controls which had been in force since 1950. Those two measures constituted the essence of what came to be known as the *Decontrol Program* of 1962.

The Decontrol Program of 1962 gave us our first experience with that deadly mix of import liberalization and devaluation.

Our application for a $300 million stabilization loan was approved by the U.S. State Department and the IMF and, pursuant to its commitment, the Macapagal administration on January 22, 1962, barely two weeks in office, devalued the peso (from the original rate of P2:$1 to P3.90:$1) and dismantled foreign currency controls.

The debt problem started there.

Q. Please explain.

A. You can see that following Decontrol in 1962 our foreign debt quadrupled by 1965. That debt has been leaping like a wild kangaroo since then.

During the time of foreign currency and import controls, our importation was rigorously controlled and was generally limited to goods classified as essential and semi-essential. Luxuries and non-essentials– like jewelry, perfume and toothpicks, to cite random examples, were either banned outright or subjected to quantitative limits.

That system enabled us to apply our earnings of dollars– mainly derived from exports– to what were essential such as industrial plants producing goods that would substitute for imports. That was how we developed the wide range of consumer industries– textile, shoes, processed food, flour, automobile assembly, electronics, household appliances and the like, none of which existed before the '50s.

Foreign currency controls also banned the use of dollars for purposes of investments overseas. For a Filipino then to invest in real estate in California or shares of stocks in Wall Street was simply unthinkable. Controls also strictly limited the right of multinational companies to ship out their profits and capital. They were forced to reinvest their profits here.

But with the dismantlement of controls, every one and anyone who had pesos could approach the Central Bank, through his bank, and apply for dollars for virtually any purpose whatsoever– except to import agricultural goods whose importation remained banned until the advent of the liberalization program of the Aquino administration.

Decontrol and the abdication of economic sovereignty to control and manage the use of the nation's limited but precious stock of dollars and international currencies.

The Decontrol Program in brief constituted a command for the country to spend and live beyond its means– and to borrow dollars for that purpose.

Because our government made a commitment to the U.S. and the IMF that it would dismantle controls in exchange for a loan of $300 million, it rendered itself powerless to regulate the outflow of dollars, even if that outflow went to finance the importation of such nonessentials as fighting cocks and basketball players, or a flood of imports that undermined the very foundation of the economy, or a sightseeing tour to see the Eiffel Tower or the Empire State building or to import call girls.

Q. But since our earnings of dollars came primarily from exports and therefore limited, how did the country manage to produce the dollars that financed transactions such as the importation of fighting cocks, basketball players and luxury items, including investments overseas, foreign travel and political junkets.

A. By borrowing.

Q. But why did we have to borrow?

A. Because that was the only way we could comply with our commitment to the IMF and the U.S. State Department that we will never impose controls on transactions that involve the use of dollars. That was the commitment our government made under the Decontrol Program in exchange for a stabilization loan of $300 million.

Q. How about the dollar remittances of Filipino overseas workers?

A. We had no such thing as overseas workers then– at least not anywhere in the magnitude that we have them now. Our main source of dollar earnings was export, and that source was limited because we hadn't yet developed the manufacturing industries that could export and compete in the international market.

Q. Why was that?

A. Because our manufacturing industries were still at their infant and learning stage and highly dependent on imported industrial raw materials, such as steel, and capital goods, namely machines and tools, in order to function.

Don't forget that our consumer and light industries were established only during the '50s.

Q. And so we had to borrow and borrow just to fulfill our commitment to the U.S. and the IMF that we shall never resort to foreign currency and import controls as we did in the '50s?

A. That's right. And that, to repeat again and again, is how the debt crisis began. It began with the Decontrol Program launched by Diosdado Macapagal in 1962 and the stabilization loan of $300 million in exchange for that program.

We have been borrowing since then– to finance the importation and other transactions that have absolutely nothing to do with developing the economy and transforming into an NIC. We have now reached the point when we simply must borrow and keep on exporting human labor just to keep the economy in motion.

Q. Borrowing dollars became a major economic activity starting in the '60s?

A. That's right. That's why during the '60s, we had a proliferation of so-called "investment banks." Their main business was to facilitate the country's effort to borrow abroad, practically for any purpose whatever. Beginning in that decade, the country borrowed dollars even for projects that weren't dollar-earning. We began to borrow dollars to make up for budgetary deficits which could have been met simply by exercising the sovereign right to print money, which is what every country does.

We borrowed dollars to finance even the foreign junkets of our politicians and government executives.

Our government was powerless to regulate those debt transactions because of the commitment not to interfere with transactions involving the use of foreign currency. In short, beginning in the '60s, the country started borrowing for just about everything except to build up industrial factories and finance the industrialization of the economy.

Q. How about the IMF conditionalities?

Those conditionalities were precisely intended to push us deeper toward a strategy of borrowing dollars to finance a development program that had nothing to do with industrialization– in fact which undermined industrialization.

Q. Do you have proof that such was the intention?

A. Yes. Recall that when Marcos tried to borrow from the IMF-WB to finance his industrial projects, his application was denied. That was crowning evidence that the IMF-WB would never allow this country to borrow dollars to finance the kind of industrialization program that made NICs of the Asian neighbors.

Q. Why do you call the debt problem the debt trap?

A. Because there's no way you can repay the debt, except to borrow to pay interest as well as principal when these become due. Our borrowings weren't used to finance and install the heavy industries that would empower us to produce our own *means of production*– the steel and machine industries that would enable us to produce consumer goods on our own and without which we shall continue to be dependent on imports for those *means of production*.

Without the heavy and machine industries, we can produce consumer goods only with machines and equipment imported from the industrial countries.

Our neighbors did the opposite. They borrowed to finance the development of their heavy and capital-goods industries, and so countries like South Korea, Malaysia, Taiwan and Indonesia can now produce their own cars, construction and earth-moving equipment and even locomotives and airplanes, armaments and even missiles, while we can't even produce a decent toy gun, much less a barrio-to-barrio missile.

The IMF conditionalities made sure, and continue to make sure, that we never develop the industrial muscle now displayed by our neighbors who pursued their development program in defiance of IMF advice.

Q. How come government after government has accepted those conditionalities?

A. Precisely because we are a neocolonial state: A supposedly sovereign nation-state run by governments that essentially function as the puppets of international powers: Specifically, of the U.S. and its proxies that are the IMF and the World Bank.

As former President Diosdado Macapagal himself said, the U.S. has been "decisive" in the choice of this nation's presidents– and therefore its governments– since independence. He should know. He was handpicked by the CIA to win the elections in 1961.

Q. How, if ever, do we get out of the debt trap?

A. Simply by repudiating the debt as the product of an unholy collusion between the U.S. and its puppets in this country.

Q. Can we afford to do that?

A. Do we have any choice– if we are to survive, as human beings?

Q. But aren't we surviving?

A. Yes. But not as human beings. Anymore than slaves survive as human beings. Are you content to survive as a slave?

WHEN A NATION ABDICATES ITS SOVER-EIGNTY TO CONTROL AND MANAGE ITS LIMITED BUT INVALUABLE STOCK OF FOREIGN CURRENCY, AS WE HAVE DONE, IT ABDICATES ITS SOVEREIGN POWER TO MANAGE ITS ECONOMY AND LEAVES THAT ECONOMY – AND THEREFORE THE LIFE OF ITS PEOPLE– TO THE MANAGEMENT OF POWERFUL BUT EXPLOITATIVE FORCES WHO RECOGNIZE NO ALLE-GIANCE EXCEPT TO MARKET FORCES, TO WHICH EVERYTHING IS SUPPOSED TO BE SACRIFICED, IN-CLUDING SOVEREIGNTY AND THE PEOPLE'S WELFARE.

THE FOREIGN DEBT IS BOTH THE SYMBOL OF OUR ECONOMIC SLAVERY AS WELL AS THE WEAPON WHICH ENABLES OTHERS TO KEEP THIS NATION ENSLAVED. AND THAT EXPLAINS THE PEOPLE'S DESCENT TO DEGENERACY.

WHEN YOU LOOK AT THE COMMON RUN OF FILIPINOS TODAY AND DIG INTO THE DEPTH OF THEIR NATURE AND THE INNER SPRINGS OF THEIR POLITICAL BEHAVIOUR– AS IN THE LAST ELEC-TIONS– YOU KNOW THAT YOU ARE NO LONGER LOOKING AT HUMAN BEINGS BUT AT DEPRIVED AND DESPERATE BEINGS SUBSISTING UNDER SUB-

HUMAN CONDITIONS AND DESPERATELY CLUTCH-
ING AT STRAWS THAT OFFER PROMISE OF
IMPROVEMENT IN THEIR LIVES.

AND SO IN THIS ONLY CHRISTIAN NATION IN
ASIA, MOTHERS MUST SELL THEIR BODIES AND
THEIR BABIES, AND THE BODIES OF THEIR DAUGH-
TERS TOO, FATHERS MUST SELL THEIR KIDNEYS,
THE POOR MUST SELL THEIR VOTES, OF COURSE,
AND SOLDIERS ARE DISPATCHED TO BATTLE WITH
TB, EVEN AS CHILD MENDICANTS BECOME AS
COMMON A SIGHT AS UNCOLLECTED GARBAGE
AND THE SICK CONTEMPLATE SUICIDE.

THAT IS THE HUMAN CONDITION OF THE VAST
MAJORITY AND THEREFORE THAT IS THE STATE OF
THE NATION.

That's the meaning of the debt crisis.

Q. And your solution is to repudiate the debt?

A. There's no other solution, moral and otherwise.

Q. What if the creditors apply sanctions?

A. They won't dare and they know why. Argentina has just
repudiated a $100 billion debt, forcing its creditors to ac-
cept a payment of 30 cents to the dollar.

WHAT WENT WRONG WITH *EDSA*: A NATION DELIVERED TO EVIL

Q. This brings me to the question now asked with increasing frequency: Just exactly what went wrong with Edsa? Why has life become much harder, and politics even more corrupt, after the people power that put to flight the Marcos dictatorship and restored democracy?

A. The answer is that the so-called *Edsa Revolution* didn't really restore democracy. What it did was to replace the personal dictatorship of Marcos with the economic dictatorship of the U.S.-IMF-WB Group. That dictatorship dictated its policies to a succession of what passed for democratically elected governments but which in fact were essentially governments that functioned as the virtual proxies or agents of the U.S.-IMF-WB.

The governments that came after Marcos made it a policy to cave in or surrender to virtually everything that the IMF and the WB demanded. And what those two agencies demanded was the total liberalization and privatization of the economy. That's what has caused the mess and the misery.

Q. Please elaborate.

A. The IMF-WB wanted: (1) total lifting of all government control over transactions involving the use of foreign currency– such as for imports, travel, transfer of capital abroad, investments overseas, and the like; (2) elimination of the government presence in the economy, except as tax collector– and even that role might be dismantled and the function of tax collection given over to private enterprise; (3) elimination of all restrictions on foreign investments so as to empower foreign investors, for example, to own land, operate public utilities and exploit natural resources, and otherwise do everything that Filipinos are allowed to do; and (4) the devaluation of the peso.

Q. Wasn't that what the Marcos dictatorship did– caved in and surrendered to the IMF-WB?

A. Initially yes. In fact, one of the reasons why the U.S. government supported his declaration of martial law was that Marcos pledged to save U.S. interests from the rising nationalism in the country. An ongoing constitutional convention was adopting resolution after resolution pointing to a forthcoming Constitution that would be radically nationalistic and even anti-American. Marcos pandered to U.S. interest in order to get the latter's support and save American business from an emerging nationalist, socialist oriented new Constitution.

But in the latter part of his term, Marcos realized that the country would have to industrialize along the path set by South Korea and Taiwan. The economy under him was growing at an annual average rate of 6 percent but that clearly wasn't enough to lift the nation from underdevelopment and poverty. It had to industrialize if it was to catch up with the neighbors and Marcos realized that.

Furthermore, throughout martial law, Marcos maintained a system of selective import controls that contravened a basic command of the IMF which wanted all controls on imports eliminated. And to compound matters, Marcos began to have the government increasingly involved in the economy. He established a national oil company, which was Petron, and government entered the business of oil exploration, which had never been done before. He nationalized the largest producer of steel products in the country, which was National Steel Corp., and was moving to establish an integrated steel mill (to produce steel products out of raw ore). By the end of the '70s, Marcos announced a program of industrialization based on the heavy industries.

Following is a description by the author Raymond Bonner of the economics to which Marcos was leading the country which eventually made him reprehensible to the U.S. government, making him a target of de-stabilization and, eventually, political decapitation.

> **Marcos was not just corrupt; he was anti-capitalist, anti-free market. He had created more government monopolies than the most dedicated of socialists.** ("Waltzing with a Dictator," TimesBooks .326)

From that passage, you can see that it wasn't so much the corruption as the fact that Marcos had turned "anti-capitalist" and "anti-free market" that concerned the Americans.

Q. And the IMF-WB didn't like that?

A. Of course the IMF-WB and the U.S. didn't like that. In setting his sights toward industrialization, Marcos was challenging the strategic geopolitical objective outlined in the *Dodds Report* to preserve the Philippines as a raw material economy. That document was the basis for what the late Claro M. Recto described as "**America's anti-industrialization policy for the Philippines.**"

And in getting the government actively involved in the economy and in maintaining a system of selective import controls, Marcos was openly defying the fundamentals of the IMF's economic ideology.

Q. You mention the economic ideology of the IMF. Please explain what that ideology is.

The ideology of the IMF:
liberal, or laissez-faire, capitalism.-

A. The IMF ideology is liberal capitalism, or what is also known as laissez-faire capitalism. It is also described aptly as unbridled capitalism.

Q. And what are the main elements of that ideology?

A. They are: (1) Absence of government regulation over the movement of goods and capital; (2) absolute supremacy of private capital– both foreign and local– in the economy; (3) no restriction on economic competition, even if that competition results in the wasteful use of resources and adverse social consequences. In brief, competition for the sake of competition even at the expense of everything else.

In terms of policies, these elements of the ideology translate into: (1) free trade; (2) privatization, meaning the government sells out state- owned enterprises to private capital, as it sold out PNB, PAL, Petron and National Steel to private capital; (3) deregulation, meaning the government doesn't attempt to regulate business activity even if the activity is one vested with public interest, like oil or the trading of basic commodities, like rice, or even the trading of the national currency.

"Market forces," under the doctrine, are supposed to be the sole determinant of prices and economic behavior, including the behavior of the peso in the currency market. Something as crucial and strategic as the national currency is to be treated like an ordinary item of commerce– like canned sardines for example - whose market value in terms of other currencies is to be dictated by "market forces," which of course include monetary speculators like George Soros.

Under laissez-faire capitalism, private capital is supposed to rule supreme in the economy and be free to do what it pleases in the name of free enterprise. The State isn't supposed to play the role of an economic activist and shouldn't commit any act or promulgate any policy that can in any way be interpreted as a form of interventionism by the State in the economy - like price controls or setting up an oil exploration company and remaining involved in the banking industry.

The god of global competitiveness.-

Under the updated version of that doctrine, the paramount good becomes what is now called *"global competitivess"*– which means that if Filipino farmers, who haven't gotten beyond sixth grade, tilling a hectare of land with primitive technology can't produce rice that can compete with rice produced on mass scale by corporate farms in the U.S. or in the industrial countries, then the government should allow Filipino farmers to starve. They don't deserve to exist because they aren't globally competitive.

Global competitiveness is the god to which everything should be subordinated and even sacrificed.

Q. But isn't that doctrine immoral– immoral because it is actually a command that government shouldn't get involved in the economy even if it is to help the poor and disadvantaged: No price control, for example, even if the price of medicine and health care and the basic services go beyond the reach of the masses; no subsidies or assistance to farmers even if the farmers are being forced by a flood of imported farm goods to abandon the only livelihood they know; no protection for domestic industries, even if imports are causing the closure of factories, and thousands of workers are being thrown in the streets, and so on?

Vatican describes IMF-WB ideology
as immoral and evil

A. Laissez-faire capitalism is immoral and evil according to the Vatican.

Q. That's news to me. What is your basis for saying that?

A. First, pick up a book authored by former Ambassador Howard Q. Dee to the Vatican titled *Mankind's Final Destiny*. In that book, Ambassador Dee recounts his conversation with the present Pope who, in no uncertain terms, said flatly that liberal capitalism is as much an evil as communism.

Q. Capitalism is an evil according to this present Pope?

A. Unbridled or laissez-faire capitalism, yes. These are passages from Ambassador Dee's book:

> In 1986, the Holy Father cautioned our country to beware of the two great evils that were afflicting humanity: communism and capitalism. . .

> The battle lines against Marxist communism were clearly defined and the enemy distinctly identifiable. It was militaristic, totalitarian and atheistic. People were controlled by fear. Not so in the battle against *unfettered capitalism* which will prove to be the real mother of all battles. . .People are seemingly free to choose but much of their lives is dictated on by an economic system controlled by an oligarchy which tends toward political patronage and monopolies.

In 1989, the present Pope delivered a speech in Copenhagen and in that speech he was quoted as saying that:

> I am fully convinced that certain forms of *modern imperialism*, which appear to be inspired by economics or politics, are in fact forms of idolatry, the worship of money, ideology, class or technology. ("Imperialists blamed for havenots' plight, Philippine Journal, June 2, 1989).

Then read the papal encyclicals which are a statement of the social doctrine of the Church and you will find that as far back as the 1930s, the Vatican already condemned liberal capitalism as the source of the problems of the world economy, which was then moving into the Great Depression.

Q. Please cite the specific encyclicals.

The *Quadragesimo Anno.-*

A. I cite the following pronouncements which appear in the corresponding encyclicals. For example, in the encyclical *Quadragesimo Anno* which was issued by Pope Pius X1 in 1931, we read the following passages:

> With regard to the civil power, Leo X111 boldly passed beyond the restrictions imposed by *liberalism,* and fearlessly proclaimed the doctrine that the civil power is more than mere guardian of law and order . . .

> . . .It is patent in our days not alone is wealth accumulated, but immense power and despotic economic domination is concentrated in the hands of a few, and that those few are frequently not the owners but only the trustees and directors of invested funds. . .

> This power become particularly irresistible when exercised by those who because they hold and control money are able also to govern credit and determine its allotment, for that reason supplying so to speak, the lifeblood of the entire economic body, and grasping as it were in their hands the very soul of production, so that no one dare breathe against their will.

The encyclical then proceeds to attribute the fact of wealth and power concentration to what it calls "**limitless free competition**"– which is precisely at the heart of the IMF-WB ideology, of which globalization is the latest expression and "global competitiveness" the highest goal.

This accumulation of power, the characteristic of the modern economic order, is a *natural result of limitless free competition* which permits the survival of those only who are the strongest which often means those who fight most relentlessly, who pay least heed to the dictates of conscience.

And then the conclusion:

Free competition and still more economic domination must be kept within just and definite limits and must be brought under the effective control of the public authority in matters appertaining to the latter's competence. . .

Q. And what about free trade?

The *Populorum Progressio.-*

A. Free trade was the subject of condemnation by the specific encyclical *Populorum Progressio*. That encyclical was issued in 1967 by Pope Paul V1. Here is what that encyclical says about free trade:

In other words, the role of free trade taken by itself, is no longer able to govern international relations. Its advantages are certainly evident when the parties involved are not affected by any excessive inequalities of economic power; it is incentive to progress and a reward for effort. That is why industrially developed countries see in it a law of justice. But the situation is no longer the same when economic conditions differ too widely from country to country; prices which are 'freely' set in the market can produce unfair results. One must recognize that it is the fundamental principle of liberalism as the rule for commercial exchange that is questioned here.

The *Mater et Magistra.-*

In *Mater et Magistra,* the affable Pope John XX111 explicitly rejected a basic element in the IMF-WB creed that the State should refrain from economic activism. That encyclical acknowledged that there are situations when the

State must be an economic activist, if only to help the economically disadvantaged, such as the nation's farmers.

These are passages in that encyclical which unquestionably establish that the principle of state economic interventionism– so anathema to the IMF-WB ideology of liberal capitalism– is part and parcel of the Church's social doctrine:

> The State, the reason for whose existence is the realization of the common good in the temporal order, cannot keep aloof from the economic world. It must be present to promote in a suitable manner the production of a sufficient supply of material goods the use of which is necessary for the practice of virtue. . . It is also its ineluctable task to contribute actively to the betterment of the condition of life of the workers. . .

> First of all, it should be affirmed that the economic order is the creation of the personal initiative of private citizens themselves working either individually or in association with such other in various ways for the prosecution of economic interests.

> But here for the reasons that our Predecessors have pointed out, the public authorities must not remain inactive if they are to promote in a proper way the productive development in behalf of social progress for the benefit of all citizens.

There isn't any question therefore that insofar as church social doctrine is concerned, the "fundamental principle" of liberal or laissez-faire capitalism is downright immoral. That fundamental principle is free, unbridled competition, not only locally but internationally: Pit the undercapitalized local industrialists against the overcapitalized multinational companies; pit the illiterate Filipino farmers against foreign corporate farms doing their farming with the aid of satellites even if that means killing the only livelihood our farmers know, and driving them to eat field rats.

And that's exactly what has been happening to this country since people power. It all began with the lunacy called import liberalization and ended up in that act of economic suicide named GATT and the WTO– without safety nets.

Why then hasn't the Church here condemned the IMF-WB?

Q. But if what you say is true, why is it that the Church here hasn't condemned the IMF-WB as well as all the governments which since Edsa have followed the commands of those two institutions?

A. Because insofar as its social doctrine is concerned, the Church here has hardly been known to follow what it preaches. The Church is much too tied up with elite and the elite want the freedom to do anything with their money, including taking their bath in Italian bathtubs, reading under the glow of Venetian chandeliers, go sightseeing around the world any old time they please and otherwise surrounding themselves with imported luxuries and gorging themselves with imported food, even if that means that the State must squander the hard-earned dollars of our overseas workers to finance the importation of non-essentials and luxuries.

The Church here obviously lives in terror of the evil incarnated in the ideology of the IMF-WB, displaying a moral cowardice which has made a caricature of the Christ who renounced Satan's offer of the power and the glory and the kingdom.

Truth is, if the Church is really serious about its social doctrines, it should from the start have condemned, and should continue to be condemning, the IMF-WB as the incarnation and assiduous promoter of a malevolent and immoral ideology that has driven millions of Filipinos to destitution and acts of desperate perversion.

As it is it has been the nationalists and the communists who have denounced, and continue to denounce, the imperialism of the IMF-WB while the Church maintains a deafening silence on the immorality of the free trade creed and creed of "global competitiveness"– preferring instead to concentrate on denouncing *jueteng* and proclaiming from the rooftops its acts of petty and inconsequential charities while issuing press releases on political issues over which it has no business interfering, just so to get itself in the papers and impress us with what it thinks is its moral ascendancy.

Q. Has there been any politician who dared to challenge the power of liberal, or laissez faire, capitalism?

Ninoy Aquino vowed to
eliminate laissez-faire
capitalism.-

A. Ninoy Aquino did– while in the confines of his prison cell. Writing his *Testament From a Prison Cell* Ninoy attributed his people's poverty to laissez-faire capitalism and vowed to eliminate it should he be placed in a position to do so.

These were Ninoy's words on laissez-faire capitalism:

> Underdevelopment is the consequence of a capitalist system that perpetuates poverty and attendant human misery, of social structures based on gross inequalities in social well-being, privilege and power. *The system must be replaced.* (p. 54)

> The dogma of laissez faire created a political situation that violated the canons of democracy. The owners of capital wielded powers so far reaching– over their employees,

over the public– without being accountable to the community, without being responsible for those whose fate they determined with their economic and political decisions. (*Testament From a Prison Cell*, p. 57).

Q. Do you think he read the papal encyclicals?

A. I see no reference to the encyclicals in his writings.

Q. And what was Ninoy's ideology?

A. These were his words in describing his ideology:

> I believe in a Christian Democratic Socialist ideology that will harmonize political freedom with social and economic equality, taking and merging the best of the primary conflicting systems– communism and capitalism. (p. 46)

Q. What did he propose to do?

A. Nationalize the basic industries, particularly the public utilities, or what he called the *"basic and strategic means of production."* This was what he said:

> Ultimately, the basic and strategic means of production must come under social ownership to ensure equitable proration of the national wealth and to safeguard the national interest. (p.53).

It is evident that if Ninoy had lived and become President, this country wouldn't have fallen under the economic dictatorship of the IMF-WB. There wouldn't have been any import liberalization and we wouldn't have joined the WTO. Public utilities and strategic industries like National Steel and Petron would never have been privatized. We can be sure that Fort Bonifacio would never have been sold to foreign real estate developers.

Ninoy would never have allowed our soldiers to be driven away from Fort Bonifacio, which has been their historic home, and driven just so to promote the interest of foreign real estate developers.

The sale of Fort Bonifacio was an act of unmitigated betrayal of the military.

Q. But if we didn't join the WTO, we would have been erased from the economic map, according to the senators who ratified GATT.

A. That's what the GATT pushers in the Senate– led by Senators Edgardo Angara and Gloria Macapagal-Arroyo– would have us believe. But look at Vietnam, China and India.

Q. What about Vietnam, India and China?

A. Vietnam isn't a member of the WTO, and not even of the IMF, and yet is doing very well. It has reduced its poverty rate by half over the last ten years while we have increased ours by at least 50 percent. It is we who have been erased from the economic map since we joined GATT and took to globalization.

Q. And what about India and China?

A. We could have joined GATT and the WTO without taking their commandments seriously or complying with them only minimally– as China and India are doing. Those nations joined GATT and WTO to take advantage of the rights and privileges that come from membership in those organizations while taking their obligations and commitments thereunder lightly, and even violating those commitments altogether. Both haven't allowed their commitments under GATT and WTO to destroy their economies.

In our case, we took to GATT and WTO and took their commandments with dead seriousness, and we continue to be dead serious about free trade and the WTO even if that has driven our people to extreme poverty and even hunger.

Q. It seems then that both Ninoy and Marcos were in a collision course with the IMF-WB and the ideology of liberal capitalism?

A. Yes. In their own respective ways and political style as well as economic philosophy Ninoy and Marcos had come to reject the very ideology incarnated by the IMF-WB. Neither believed in the ideology of liberal capitalism and both were apparently set to dismantle it in the Philippines.

In the case of Marcos, he was resisting the IMF-WB through his dictatorship and he was clearly moving toward a state-directed industrialization, state capitalism and economic controls. Ninoy would have done it through the ways of democratic socialism. .

Q. But wasn't Marcos corrupt?

A. Here we go again. You must stop listening to the Church, the Opus Dei, the U.P. economists and the Makati Business Club, all of whom want us to believe that at the bottom of the hunger is corruption– and not the treason of our policies, which they have promoted either actively or by their silence.

Can you name me one single human institution or organization that isn't corrupt? Isn't the Church corrupt? Isn't the Makati business community corrupt– or more aptly said, isn't there high corruption in those high places too?

WHY NINOY AND MARCOS HAD TO GO

Q. And so both Ninoy and Marcos had to go– because they were both out to dismantle the liberal capitalism incarnated by the IMF-WB?

A. Both had to go because both had become obstacles to the absolute economic dictatorship of the IMF-WB and, eventually, of the globalists. With both Marcos and Ninoy out of the way, the IMF-WB were able to establish virtually absolute dominion over the economy and to push us eventually to the WTO and globalization.

With Ninoy and, subsequently, Marcos gone, free traders and globalists took charge of the economy through the U.P. economists, ranking elements of the Opus Dei and the Makati business community. They started with import liberalization under Corazon C. Aquino and climaxed into GATT, the WTO and globalization under Fidel V. Ramos, Joseph Estrada and Gloria Macapagal-Arroyo.

Since Edsa we have been living under the spell and dominion of the evil that resides in unbridled capitalism and free trade, and that sums up the matter.

A final word about free trade:
The economic basis of colonialism.

What shouldn't be forgotten as we conclude this discussion is that free trade, which is an essential ingredient of globalization and today's liberal capitalism, has always functioned as the economic basis of colonialism. It is the economic relation, forced by the colonial powers on their colonies– as when Britain forced it on her American colonies and when the U.S. in turn forced it on the Philippines– that enabled the colonizing powers to exploit their colonies and preserve the latter in a state of underdevelopment.

As the late Salvador Araneta succinctly put it during the debate on the free trade provision of the Bell Trade Act of 1946:

> Free trade between an industrial country and an agricultural country is to the detriment of the agricultural country. There is no country which has been able to become industrialized without having had to protect its industries.
>
> Free trade means no industrialization for the Philippines. It means a backward Philippines that will be little more than an economic dependency of the United States, serving in that regard the function of a vegetable garden to an industrial state. (see Araneta "Economic Reexamination of the Philippines").

As for the popes, this is what they have to say of free trade according, to the Rev. Pedro V. Salgado, O.P. in his book *Social Encyclicals*:

> The popes tell us that free trade leads to the grabbing of Third World wealth by the rich industrial nations.

Q. Your conclusion then is that Edsa went wrong because it delivered us to the ideology of laissez-faire capitalism and free trade, which the popes have condemned as evil?

A. Yes.

Q. What do we do then to be delivered from the evil and get out of the hunger and the mess?

A. Let's discuss that in the sequel to this primer.

www.ingramcontent.com/pod-product-compliance
Lightning Source LLC
Chambersburg PA
CBHW071200280526
45787CB00002B/548